She Fights

BECOMING A WOMAN OF WISDOM, WORTH AND WHOLENESS

CAVALINE COLQUHOUN

SHE FIGHTS. Copyright © 2025. Cavaline Colquhoun. All Rights Reserved.

Printed in the United States of America.

No portion of this book may be reproduced, stored in a retrieval system, or transmitted in any form or by any means, except for brief quotations in printed reviews, without the prior written permission of DayeLight Publishers or Cavaline Colquhoun.

ISBN: 978-1-966723-19-6 (paperback)

Scripture quotations marked "KJV" are taken from the Holy Bible, King James Version (Public Domain).

Scripture quotations marked (NIV) are taken from the Holy Bible, New International Version®, NIV®. Copyright © 1973, 1978, 1984 by Biblica, Inc.™ Used by permission of Zondervan. All rights reserved worldwide.

Scripture quotations marked "NASB" are taken from the New American Standard Bible®, Copyright © 1960, 1962, 1963, 1968, 1971, 1972, 1973, 1975, 1977, 1995 by The Lockman Foundation. Used by permission.

Scripture quotations marked (NLT) are taken from the Holy Bible, New Living Translation, copyright © 1996, 2004, 2007 by Tyndale House Foundation. Used by permission of Tyndale House Publishers, Inc., Carol Stream, Illinois 60188. All rights reserved.

Scripture quotations marked "NKJV" are taken from the New King James Version. Copyright © 1982 by Thomas Nelson, Inc. Used by permission. All rights reserved. Bible text from the New King James Version® is not to be reproduced in copies or otherwise by any means except as permitted in writing by Thomas Nelson, Inc., Attn: Bible Rights and Permissions, P.O. Box 141000, Nashville, TN 37214-1000.

Scripture quotations marked "ESV" are from the ESV Bible® (The Holy Bible, English Standard Version®), copyright © 2001 by Crossway Bibles, a publishing ministry of Good News Publishers. Used by permission. All rights reserved.

Acknowledgments

I would like to express my thanks and appreciation to Jehovah the Almighty God, who, through the Holy Spirit, gave me the fortitude and wisdom to write this book.

Profound love and gratitude to my beloved parents, Desmond and Millicent Johnson, and my amazing siblings, Dwight, Dale, Sharline, Hustan, Thelka, and Raymond Johnson. My loving cousins, who lived with us, Linval and Angela Sewell, Garfield, Debbie, and Troy Beason, were a bedrock, a solid foundation that set the stage for my life.

Deep appreciation to my beloved Aunt Norma McPhil, who opened her home and shared her bed when I was homeless. My grandmother, Alvira Pollock, encouraged me to strive for excellence. Aunt Elsada (Cecile) Stewart for her support when I needed her the most. My Godparents, Michael and Shiela Murray, who rescued me from atrocities and nursed me back to mental wellness when I was not able to care for myself. My uncle, Bishop Dr. Fedlyn, and my Aunt, Esmine Beason, who provided the first school fee down payment, and Alvida Gordon, who contributed to my nursing career.

Special thanks to my spiritual midwife, Aunt Pamela Johnson, my mentor and counselor, who believed in me and gave me her nursing badge, nursing scissors, an hourglass, and a postcard that read. *"Cut your way through life. Don't stop until you graduate from Nursing School. Be on time all the time, and when you graduate, God forbid, I should pass, please return the nursing badge to my daughter, Sharon Johnson."* My longest best friends, Camille Gordon-Dorah and Eulalee Wilis-Roberts who, stood with me through tough times and deep waters. My phenomenal, heaven-sent daughter, Camille Gray, and my grandchildren, Isaiah and Alana, to whom I owe so much. My church family labored in prayer for my health and well-being. My staff and colleagues are second to none.

Finally, my darling husband, Rev. Christopher Colquhoun, my priest and a "good gift" for his ceaseless prayers and unwavering support, and to everyone who has impacted my life.

Thank you.

Foreword

"The righteous cry out, and the Lord hears them; he delivers them from all their troubles. The Lord is close to the brokenhearted and saves those who are crushed in spirit." (Psalm 34:17-18 - NIV).

Your story matters. Even amid chaos, your voice, your presence, and your fight all carry profound meaning. You may not immediately see the impact of your perseverance, but rest assured, you are lighting a path for others who will follow in your footsteps.

When Cavaline asked me to write the foreword for her book, "She Fights: Becoming a Woman of Wisdom, Worth and Wholeness," I immediately thought of Psalm 34:17-18. This scripture speaks beautifully to the heart of her message: God hears our cries, sees our struggles, and draws close to us in times of brokenness and despair.

I believe deeply in the importance of women sharing their stories. It is not only empowering but healing. Sharing our experiences allows us to reclaim our voices, process our journeys, and assert control over our narratives—especially in circumstances where we might have felt silenced. This act of courage helps us and those around us find strength, peace, and renewed hope.

Becoming a woman of wisdom, worth, and wholeness is a powerful affirmation that I hold dear: "I am a woman of worth and wisdom—created with purpose, guided by truth, and anchored in grace. My value is not defined by the world but by the One who made me. I walk with dignity, speak with discernment, and love with intention. I grow through every season, and through me, others find strength, peace, and light."

As you read Cavaline's heartfelt words and reflections, may you be encouraged that God is always with you, providing constant comfort and strength. You never face hardships alone; there is a higher power walking beside you, guiding your steps and empowering you to move forward confidently, no matter what life brings.

Keep going—your journey is valuable, your story is powerful, and your fight is worth it.

With heartfelt encouragement,

Karen Smith
NY Women's Ministries Director

Table of Contents

Acknowledgments iii
Foreword v
Introduction 9
Chapter 1: Is The Fight Worth It? 15
Chapter 2: Why Should I Pursue Wisdom? 45
Chapter 3: Is Wisdom By Choice or By Chance (How to Walk in Wisdom) 63
Chapter 4: How Much Are You Worth? 77
Chapter 5: How Does Your Self-Worth Influence Your Net Worth? 97
Chapter 6: Can I Really Be Whole? 111
Chapter 7: Discover Your Hidden Treasure 133
Chapter 8: Power of Resilience In The Fight 155
Conclusion: Your Turning Point 171
About the Author 177
References 179

Introduction

The compilation of this book was birth from the Holy Spirit, as mentioned in the acknowledgement. I was sitting in my office, writing another book, the topic of which was undecided. When the Holy Spirit gave me the topic "She Fights," I quickly searched the internet to see if there was a published book with that title. I perused various sites but to no avail. I thought, *"God would never give me a topic for a book that someone had already published."* So, I started writing quickly as the Holy Spirit instructed me to write. My spirit was on fire as I typed the words that flowed continuously through my heart. I never wanted to stop, not even to relieve myself, lest I lose my train of thought.

"She Fights" is about who you can become in Christ, knowingly or unknowingly. This book is about a little girl who was determined in her heart to achieve her dreams and desires and be a destiny changer, even though the situation and circumstances around her reflected otherwise. I fought long and hard with low self-esteem, fear, doubt, lack, and insecurity.

Growing up, there were few role models and even fewer people to confide in, as they would often say one thing and do the opposite. That was a significant challenge for me and a major hurdle to overcome, so I tried to do things my way, which marked the beginning of a whole new scenario.

I was always a "Jesus girl," as my relatives and people in the community would call me. As children, we had to attend church every day of the week and twice on Sundays. On Saturdays, we helped with the cleaning of the sanctuary, and that was not up for discussion.

The barrier of protection was removed from us when our mom migrated to the city for gainful employment. This opened a can of worms for us, especially for me, as the eldest girl. My role quickly changed from that of a child to a caregiver, causing inadequacy and a lack, which was to my disadvantage; at least, that was what I thought. I soon forgot what the scripture said about being a child of God. I felt burdened, unloved, unwanted, neglected, and undeserving. I was giving care that I desperately needed myself as a child.

I was unable to manage the task assigned, and after graduating from secondary school, I migrated to the city with the intention of continuing my education and seeking employment. That move was a rude awakening. Unfortunately, things never worked as planned because I was naive, immature, and inexperienced, believing that the little rural community was like the rest of the world. I experienced culture shock and was deeply disappointed when I realized that the structure, culture, and people in the city were not the same as those in the quiet little rural community where I grew up, where everyone knew each other; it was like night and day. I felt lost, but I was determined that I would not return to my birth parish and definitely not to my community.

I moved from house to house, job to job, in search of a home, employment, and love. I was backslidden and became a mother. I had entered into a marriage that I did not belong to because the Holy Spirit told me three times "no" and that I should run for my life. A few years later, I became homeless, helpless, and hopeless, with no sense of direction. It was there that I had an encounter with the Lord, and my life has never been the same since.

During my childhood years, adults in the community, including teachers and spiritual leaders, would tell my parents and me that there was something special about me. They looked at each other affirmingly, which made me feel uncomfortable and led me to think that something was wrong. When I behaved like my peers, they would scold me, saying that I knew better and should do better without correcting the others.

I felt like people were picking on me; even strangers would point me out of a crowd and say there was just something different about me. I never believed them because nothing they had said over the years had come to realization. I could not see myself as a registered nurse, ministering to the needs of my patients, and becoming a pastor's wife or first lady, ministering to women who would become "Women of Wisdom, Worth, and Wholeness."

Nothing made sense, and not even a piece of the puzzle was in view. My life was in disarray, with no sense of direction. Things were against the grain at high tide, with no assurance that the promise of God still stands. Each time I tried to do something productive, I was told it was not good enough and that I could have done better. I was attacked in the corridor and dragged into one of the side rooms at work and was asked who I thought I was. They claimed to have been there for years and struggled to advance up the ranks, and I just appeared from nowhere with little qualification and no experience, wanting to fill a position; it didn't work like that. Looking back, I realized that God was preparing and setting me up for the day when I finally embraced my calling and surrendered all to the God who called me to be purpose. I could not die where I fought, for I am a masterpiece, a destiny child, with a clear blueprint that strategically placed me here for such a time as this. The war was fierce, and the pain and suffering were real, but so was God's grace and mercy.

I come from humble beginnings; born in a small farming district in rural Jamaica, where I was raised by the community. My parents were Christians: Dad was a deacon and farmer, and Mom was a Sunday school teacher, evangelist, cook, and seamstress for the community. They were taught the scriptures and were expected to live the scriptures. The Bible was my favourite book, but I was afraid to read certain chapters as it convicted me to change my ways of living to Christlikeness.

As the third of seven children and the first daughter, I collaborated with my mom and helped with domestic chores while she operated her cook shop or grocery shop on the main street, just a few meters from our house, to support the family. They had extra mouths to feed when my cousins visited during the Easter, Summer, and Christmas holidays, but even more so when their visits became permanent. The pressures of life were overwhelming, and money was scarce. As a result, situations at home became increasingly complicated, forcing my mother to make a difficult decision: either leave her young children to seek employment in the city or stay in the impoverished conditions that were both embarrassing and belittling.

I wanted to be rich, travel the world, and help those people whom God wanted me to assist. I believed that money was the only way to fulfill all my desires. I believed that since the family was not wealthy, I had to study hard to earn good grades and climb the academic ladder, find a rich man, or win the lottery. Although I was a Christian, I was not truly relying on God because He was not moving at the pace I had hoped, and I wanted things to happen immediately. As a result, I did everything I should not have and went where I did not belong, hurting myself and others and suffering the consequences thereof.

This is my story.

CHAPTER 1

Is The Fight Worth It?

1. The Battle (Tragedy and Triumph)
2. Listening to the Wrong Voice (Adding Fire to Fury)
3. Overcoming the Fight in the Presence of God

CHAPTER 1 SUMMARY

Since the fall of man, there has been a continual battle between good and evil, right and wrong, light and darkness, and other opposing forces.

There has always been a struggle to excel and succeed and to accomplish what you have set out to do.

The more you try to do good, evil presents itself and causes hindrance, creating challenges that make it difficult to focus on the things that are important to you.

To overcome this fight, you need to tune your ears and heart to the voice of the Lord, and He will teach you the strategies to overcome the plans and tricks of the adversary, for this fight is worth winning.

THE BATTLE (TRAGEDY AND TRIUMPH)

A battle is defined as a sustained fight between large, organized armed forces (Oxford, 2025)—a hostile encounter between opposing forces (Merriam Dictionary). The origin comes from the Latin word "battuere," meaning "to beat," and "bataille," an old French word that refers to military or gladiatorial exercises (Oxford, 2025). A battle occurs when there is a disagreement or dispute between parties that cannot be resolved peacefully, resulting in a fight to achieve the desired outcome. It is simply negotiating through violence. Conflict is always costly, resulting in catastrophes and casualties. The battle began on the day of creation, when God created man from the earth (dust) and breathed His breath (the Spirit) into man, making him a living soul. The enemy of the soul deceived the first soul, Adam, and warfare with the spirit and the flesh, good and evil ensued (see Genesis 3).

The battle continued at conception when my dad's sperm had to do a sprint race against gravity in rough terrains of unfavorable conditions that could cause its demise to reach my mom's ovum for fertilization to take place for me to be in existence.

My mom shared with us that when she was pregnant with me, the pregnancy was fairly good; however, the enemy tried to rob me of clothing (protection and wealth) before I was born. When her neighbour's daughter went into labour, she had to give her the baby clothes she made for me; she was later compensated for the baby clothes. At the age of eleven, I was beaten and my right ear bitten off by the same neighbour's daughter. It caused me to miss the first chance to sit the common entrance examination, a prerequisite for high school. I was certain I would pass on the first sitting to attend the most prestigious high school in our parish. My teachers encouraged me that if I continued to pursue my passion for education, I would surely become whatever I wanted to be in life.

I am from a small rural farming community in St. Mary, Jamaica, where I lived with my parents, siblings, and cousins. We did not have basic commodities like electricity and running water, but we were safe and happy, and we never went to bed hungry. At first, I did not know we were that poor because members of the community would ask our parents for ground provisions and cow's milk every week. All seemed well until, at the age of fifteen, my mom migrated to the city for gainful employment, leaving me, the eldest girl, to manage the home. It was one of the hardest things I had to face as a teenager; it was like walking on a hamster wheel with no sense of direction because there was so much at stake, and I did not know how or where to start.

First, I cried, and I cried, and then I cried some more, but I quickly realized that my mother was not coming back, and my siblings were totally dependent on me. I felt forsaken and disappointed and blamed myself for thinking that if I had done more to help my mother with the grocery store and cook shop, it would have been more profitable, and she would never have had to leave in the first place. I reminisced about the days when she asked me to stay home from school to help her cook and serve because I was more responsible than my older brothers. We would cook and serve dozens of workers from the Boxing Plant, where bananas were prepared for export, every Friday and Saturday. I remember one Thursday evening, when I was at home studying, my mom told me to put down the books and help her prepare the menu for the previous day, as it promised to be a big workday, and she wanted to take advantage of the sale. I placed the books on the table and went to season the meat, cut the vegetables, and manually grated dozens of dried coconuts using a grater. We would extract the juice from the grated coconuts and add it to red beans or gungo peas to make rice and peas, as well as a stew combined with a variety of red meats. We use the waste from grated coconuts to make toto, a delicious pastry. The customers loved my mom's cooking, and they kept coming back for more. I sympathized with my mom and did my best to help her, but all I really wanted to do was learn and excel in my exams.

One Friday morning, I got up early, awakened by the noise of the pots and pans. My mom was ready to go to the cookshop, so she took me with her. In no time, the breakfast was done and served. I washed the dirty plates and utensils because they were washable. I hurriedly helped to start lunch and kept asking the workers the time because I wanted to go sit my exams. All seemed fine until it was time for me to go to school, which was an hour's drive from home.

My mom insisted, and I stayed to help for the rest of the day. At the time, I was determined to sit the exams, which was the most important thing in the world to me; nothing else mattered. So, I dressed for school, and when I went to collect my bus fare, my mom used a dirty piece of cloth that we had used to dye the floor red when cleaning and hit me across my back. Writing these words, my eyes welled with tears. I ran away as fast as I could from the scene, cleaned myself, and on the way to school, I had my book bag on my back. As I hurried, I would look for familiar vehicles that would take me for free because I didn't have bus fare, and the few public passenger transportation options would not take me for free unless I gave in to their demands. I walked the five-mile journey to school, taking shortcuts and running when no one was visible.

When I arrived at school, one of the exams had already started, and the form teacher asked why I was late, dirty, and sweaty. I told her I had to walk because I did not have bus fare. I told her my mom told me not to attend school, but I insisted, and she hit me with the floor cloth. I could see that I had caused a distraction, but everyone settled down quickly and proceeded to complete the exam. Those grades were among the best I had received in that class. Every time I am about to accomplish something great, obstacles always arise, but when I persist, the outcomes are rewarding.

Growing up, I was a sickly child. I suffered from respiratory illnesses such as cold, asthma, pneumonia, dengue, and late teen chicken pox. I was allergic to penicillin injections, pollen, and honey. I never liked meat, but I loved gravy and everything fried except eggs. I was underweight for my age, so the doctor and nurses at the clinic encouraged mom to give me more food, including milk, because they thought she was not feeding me, which was not the case; I was a fussy eater. Mom was happy to serve me milk because my dad would carry home a bucket of cow's milk from the farm every day. Mom would give me the cream of the milk to eat, and every time she did, I would vomit and scratch a lot. She would heat the cow's milk in a saucepan, and when it started to boil, she would remove it from the heat and allow it to cool. Then, she would remove the cream that had settled on top, which was rich in fats. She would repeat the process until she achieved a required amount. She would add milk to mashed potatoes, pumpkin, and banana and use it to boil porridge, insisting that I eat it. Mom said I turned my mind from milk because I did not like it. Yes, that is a fact. I did not like milk because milk did not like me, and I still do not like it.

Mom wanted me to be well, like my other siblings and cousins, and to eat so I could gain more weight. Every week, she would purchase a can of Milo, which is like hot chocolate, just for me, not because she could afford it, but to disguise the taste of the milk so I could eat healthier. The doctors threatened her to take better care of me because of my poor health and the frequent doctor's visits. So, she would try everything she knew to make the food more palatable for me because I didn't like vegetables. The more mom forced me to consume dairy products, the more I vomited, until one day, I vomited blood and was rushed to the hospital, where I was diagnosed with an ulcerated stomach and eczema. It was then the doctors found out that I was lactose intolerant. They told my mother to stop giving me dairy products altogether. I have been fighting sicknesses all my life: childhood, adolescence, and now an adult, but God has been faithful.

I have been fighting all my life to stay healthy, to get a job, to keep the job, and to find love.
I fought to protect my sanity when I was cheated of my home, job, marriage, and family.

I fought to make tough decisions, even when it cost my happiness.

I fought to make connections with relatives who made it clear that they denounced me and did not want to speak or associate with me ever again.

The day I started this book, "She Fights," and every day since has been a live event of a fighting match. I had to care for the sick one after the other in the family, and I was the main caregiver; then, to make matters worse, I became ill and could not leave the house for weeks only to receive medical treatment.

I kept reminding myself that I was going to finish this book within the allotted time schedule and not a day over. God had me on this assignment, and I cannot die; nothing will happen to prevent me from completing, publishing, and launching. I could literally see myself on stages and in different arenas, sharing my book and the story behind it.

I recall that I started drafting a book, but it all fell through due to sickness, procrastination, tragedy, disappointment, and distractions.

I felt like I was actually pregnant. During the months of writing, I experienced severe back pains and numbness in my lower limbs and both hands. I had to wear braces on my hands because of bilateral carpel tunnel syndrome, and the pain restricted me from writing and typing. I could not sit up, stand up, or even lie down for prolonged periods of time without disabling pain.

I would experience side effects from the medications that the doctor prescribed for the back pain.

I was referred to the orthopedic/spinal surgeons by my primary doctor for care, who requested tests to confirm or rule out their suspicions. The results of the X-ray, CT scan, and MRI may not reflect my likeness, but I believe the great, big, wonderful God, who is Jehovah Rapha, is still in the healing business. I know God provides medicine and medical personnel to improve healthcare, but I have been in this situation before. I underwent spinal surgery ten years ago, and I did not wish for history to repeat itself because the healing process is long and disabling. I was unable to concentrate due to the side effects of medications, and I needed to focus on God's business and ministry through this book.

My people, as the Lord told me in a vision, and I quote, *"Cavaline Colquhoun, receive your people."* I am still in awe and questioning whether I heard correctly and how to interpret it. The last time I heard that line was God telling Moses to "tell your people," which meant Moses' people...." (see Exodus 32:7). Since then, I have had a Jeremiah moment, *"I feel like fire shut up within my womb."* I had to write this book; I must because you are waiting to receive the Living Word of God, which transcends and connects to your spirit, increasing your faith and transforming you from the inside out to take action. Just as the Holy Spirit is transforming and equipping me, you too will experience a new mindset that will change your perspective on yourself and what the Lord is waiting to reveal to you in a practical way through this book.

The struggles, rejections, failures, and isolation in my life were real and forced me to turn to God because there was absolutely no one else who could help me but God. All doors were closed, or may I say, shut, and at times, just walls were staring at me. God wanted my attention so badly that He allowed everything around me to close so I could acknowledge His presence. He has always been there, even when I had backslidden and gone after the things of this world.

I asked God why He saved me from the death and hell that I was exposed to. I was wrestling in my spirit about what my divine purpose was because although I had accomplished what many women would never achieve, I wasn't at ease. I felt unfulfilled and needed to do something more, and it wasn't about material gain or pleasure. God said to me in a vision on October 2, 2021 @ 4:44 am *"Cavaline Johnson, I have preserved you for My righteousness, and I have protected you for My glory."*

Since then, I have stopped complaining and grumbling in my spirit, but I give God thanks and praise for who He is and for His excellent greatness (see Psalm 150:2). This has increased my faith in God as I reminisce about how He has been working out His purpose for my good. Knowing that it was in the time of weakness, vulnerability, and unexpecting that God showed up on my behalf and delivered again.

I saw Christians living a double-standard life. They were saying one thing and doing something else. But when an individual I respected was caught in a compromised position, due to a lack of trust and not relying on God to take care of my needs, I gave in to my desires. One thing led to another, and I was way over my head in a relationship that I didn't belong in. Realizing the pain I had caused a particular family, I felt guilty and concerned, and a feeling of remorse weighed heavily on my shoulders for years. I asked how I had reached that point when I should have known better because my parents and grandmother instilled moral, ethical, and biblical principles in me. I was a Christian, for heaven's sake, Holy Ghost-filled, water-baptized, but was not living a holy, consecrated life that was pleasing to God. Fighting in my own weakness of shame and guilt was always a come between me and God. I felt like how I was treated when I was among my brethren. When they thought I did well, I was accepted, but the moment they found out that I messed up, I was ostracized and condemned, and not even spoken to.

LISTENING TO THE WRONG VOICE: ADDING FIRE TO FURY

We are living in the Information Age, also known as the computer age, where there is a shift from traditional industries, such as manufacturing, education, and specific segments of the retail sector, among others. There is a shift from a manual labour force and machinery to a more economically based information technology, where tasks are completed and products are produced at a rapid pace with multiple outcomes. People are competing to be heard, and as a result, there are multiple sources of attraction and distraction. As of 2025, over two billion people interact with reels each month, with more than 200 billion reels played on Facebook and Instagram daily. Approximately 500,000 hours of video content are uploaded every hour.

AI has its place, and we are grateful for the wisdom God has given humans to analyze, predict, and complete complex tasks in a timely manner, advancing production and saving lives.

Because information is readily available, the general public has access at their fingertips; however, there are false voices that are not correct, not truthful, and not intended for adequate growth and development. As a result, there needs to be a juncture where the vulnerable members of society are alerted and protected from the risks and dangers they may face.

The culture in the education system has undergone significant changes, along with the curriculum and the content of reading materials, where once age-appropriate information was provided and enforced. Now, you are unable to detect the difference between elementary school and high school or college as it relates to content, and that in itself is quite alarming.

I agree that information once considered acceptable and lawful, which was taught to us, is now described as outdated and no longer relevant to the current generation. For example, we no longer use critical thinking to solve problems and interpret correctly what scriptures say about how to live and for what to live.

We need to be cautious about the things we expose ourselves to and should be very selective about the information we take in. Wisdom will teach us who and what to listen to. Remember, our ear is like a womb; whatever we listen to, we will conceive, reproduce, and give birth to. Jesus told His disciples to, *"Pay attention to what you hear: with the measure you use, it will be measured to you and still more will be added to you" (Mark 4:24 – ESV).* The more you actively listen to the Word of God, the more you will understand and receive; then you will know how to apply them.

With the massive inflow and availability of data, there have been numerous voices competing for your attention. Regardless of the concerns, queries, and thoughts you may have, information of all kinds is available on the global web to provide answers, advice, and suggestions. Once you turn on your computer or enter a search engine on your phone, information jumps out at you from all angles, and it may not be relevant to what you are interested in.

You need to be mindful of the source you pay attention to because some are not credible for edification, reproof, and sound doctrine, which will teach you how to live ethically and responsibly in your family, community, and the world around you.

Whatever voice you focus on will help shape the core of your thought process and decision-making. Paul reminded us in Philippians 4:8, *"Finally, brothers and sisters, whatever is true, whatever is honorable, whatever is right, whatever is pure, whatever is lovely, whatever is commendable, if there is any excellence and if anything, worthy of praise, think about these things." (NASB2020).*

The word "ear" is found in the middle of the word "heart," and the ear is the way to the heart. So, if you want someone's heart, just listen to them because out of the heart flows the issues of life (see Proverbs 4:23). Our thoughts, feelings, and actions are influenced by what we allow into our hearts.

Hearing is considered the fastest sense of the body due to the auditory nerve, which sends signals to the brain at a speed of about 1,000 feet per second. This is much faster than the optic nerve responsible for vision, which sends signals at about 300 feet per second. Bear in mind that the other senses, though different, are just as important in how information is received.

So, guard your mind, for whatever the mind conceives, the heart receives because they both intertwine. Sometimes, the heart is referred to as the mind; they are used interchangeably, as you cannot engage the mind without involving the heart (see Psalm 73:21; Matthew 12:34).

"My child, pay attention to my words, listen attentively to my sayings. Do not let them depart from your sight, guard them within your heart, for they are life to those who find them and heal the entire body. Guard your heart with all vigilance, for from it are the sources of life." (Proverbs 4:20-23 – NLT).

CAV'S STORY

I remember we went camping at the Blue Mountain, which is the longest range and highest point in Jamaica, with a Peak of 2256 m (7402 ft), the third-highest island in the Caribbean. There were tour guides, as well as three soldiers from the Jamaica Defense Force (JDF), who were very familiar with the different sites and scenes. They would give us instructions on how to manage the terrains of the mountain range. For those individuals who wanted to climb to the pinnacle of the mountain, strict instructions were given, along with a demonstration on how to reach the peak. We were informed that the track to the peak was too steep for vehicular traffic, so only the essential items listed for the trip were requested to be packed in each person's backpack. Each group was told to trust and follow their leader, not to turn to the right or to the left, but to listen attentively to the instructions on the journey.

I noticed that the trips to the peak were only done at night, and the campers went and complied with all the rules they were instructed to follow. Unfortunately, I was unable to go to the peak because I was the only nurse on site and had injuries to attend to. When the campers returned to base and shared their experience, some complained about the distance and steepness, but they were all ecstatic about the beautiful sight of the city below and the lights displayed in Cuba, which is approximately 302.42 miles (486.69 km) from Jamaica. They wouldn't have traded the experience for the world.

The tour guides commended the happy campers for their obedience and offered to take them again, as they had requested, until they described the narrow track they had ventured on. The campers responded that if they had known the risks involved, they would never have gone there in the first place. I realized that the tour guides chose nights when the place was dark so the campers would not be distracted by the height seen on either side of the narrow tract that led to the peak of the mountain. Few of the campers had a phobia and would panic, making the trip less adventurous and unforgettable.

I shared this story to say that you really need to pay special attention to the voice you listen to because it will either make you or break you. It will allow you to step out of your comfort zone and take risks that will enable you to challenge your abilities and push past your fears and insecurities. This will remove barriers and limitations, revealing your purpose and how to maximize your true potential.

God wants us to listen to His voice and obey His Word.

"In the beginning was the Word, and the Word was with God, and the Word was God." (John 1:1 - NKJV).

God spoke, and everything came into existence, including the heavens, earth, and seas with their contents (see Genesis 1). All things were made through Him, and without Him, there was not anything made that was made (see John 1:3). When the earth was completed, God said, *"Let us make man in Our likeness." (Genesis 1:26).* God, the Father, God, the Son, and God, the Holy Spirit; the three persons of the divine trinity were in operation.

So, God created the first human being, named Adam, and from Adam's rib, God created a woman to be his helpmeet, whom He called Eve (meaning "life-giver"). She was the first woman on earth, and God said it was very good. God planted a garden and instructed Adam to keep it and to eat from all the trees in the garden except the tree of the knowledge of good and evil. God also gave them the earth to subdue and have dominion over it. Then, the serpent, the subtle beast of the field, came to Eve and said, *"You will not surely die. For God knows that in the day you eat of it your eyes will be opened, and you will be like God, knowing good and evil." (Genesis 3:4-5 - NKJV).* The enemy refused to tell the whole truth, and so doubt came to their minds, and they disobeyed God.

The enemy, satan, has always been undermining the power and majesty of God as Creator by competing for the loyalty and devotion of human beings. Since the fall, there has been a spiritual warfare in the world where God is seeking after men to turn away from evil to a life of perfect peace and harmony with God and to resist evil and lies.

This battle is much bigger than us; it belongs to the Lord. God said that you are fighting from a place of victory, and that settled it. All we need to do is trust God and take Him at His Word. This journey of life is like a "fighting match";

there are rules and instructions that govern the fight. Your opponent is after your soul to steal, kill, and destroy you (see John 10:10).

In the match, you are instructed to always face your opponent and never turn your back to your enemy. God left Adam and Eve, and in a split second, the enemy presented himself and deceived Eve, who in turn convinced her husband to eat, and as a result, sin entered the perfect world.

Do not let the enemy entertain you. He does not like you, and you shouldn't like him either. He cannot be tamed. The Bible said to shun the very appearance of evil (see 1 Thessalonians 5:22).

During your struggle, you may feel overwhelmed by the pain, shame, disappointment, and great expectations of the spectators, which may include your family and loved ones. But regardless of your feelings, you are in it to win it and to be declared champion. Your opponent does not have the same intentions and may even be more desperate than you because the enemy's sole purpose is to kill you. So, you need to focus on your **"why."** When you are fighting, remember that the enemy is deceiving and conniving; he is a trickster and the father of lies. He breaks every rule of the match, biting, kicking, and head-butting and using every move that is illegal. At no time should you let down your guard because he has no mercy, nor does he have a thread of honesty in him. Never trust your enemy; always follow the rules. Always prepare for the fight, know your opponent, dress your mind and body, and, most importantly, be unpredictable both on defense and offense. You may be hurting and bleeding in the ring, but keep on fighting and know who is with you. God never lost a battle, so you are fighting from a place of victory. Give it all you've got; never throw in the towel because winners never quit. God's strength is perfect in your weakness (see 2 Corinthians 12:9).

The enemy might be beating the daylight out of you; just muster the courage and give him that uppercut that will land him flat on his back to never rise again in the match. When you are in battle, you should not show sympathy because it is not a pity party; it's either you leave standing or you die. Do not let the enemy know the pain and hurt you are feeling. The enemy is not your friend, and you should not feel comfortable around him.

We know the story of Samson and Delilah. Samson was a Nazarite from the womb because the Holy Spirit told his mother, Zorah, during conception that Samson would be a Nazarite who would consecrate himself to the service of the Lord. As a Nazarite, he was expected to be holy and live a life of purity during the separation period of his vow, which could last 7 days, 30 days, or be a permanent lifetime vow. He vowed to God to abstain from wine, cutting/shaving of his hair, and coming into contact with dead bodies (see Judges 14:9 and Numbers 6:1-9). Samson was an Israelite judge and a tribal leader who had authority in Gaza, fighting against the Philistines. He was a strong warrior who defeated his enemies, including killing lions with his bare hands.

Samson received supernatural strength through the power of the Holy Spirit when he made a covenant with God. Samson has never been shaved since he was born, and if he shaved his head, his strength would leave him, and he would be as weak as any other man (see Judges 16:17).

Then Samson met a Philistine harlot and made her his mistress, and the lord of the Philistines offered 1100 pieces of silver if she could entice him and let him reveal the secret to his strength. Delilah did as she was bribed and asked Samson where his strength lay, but each time, she tried to tie him, and she told him the Philistines were upon him; he would break whatever she used to tie him. Delilah was sad and nagged him daily, saying, *"How can you say, 'I love you,' when your heart is not with me? You have mocked me these three times, and have not told me where your great strength lies." (Judges 16:15 - NKJV)*. So, she persistently pressured him for days until he finally gave in and revealed the secret of his strength to her. Samson was deceived, believing that he could trust Delilah in spite of her being a Philistine woman. She cut his hair and bound him. The Philistines plucked out his eyes, and he became their slave for years.

Samson regrew his hair, and he cried unto God and asked to regain his strength. The Lord gave Samson back his strength, and he pushed over the pillars of the Philistine god, Dagon's, temple, killing himself and thousands of the Philistines (see Judges 16:1-31).

The Bible instructs us to love our enemies and do good to those who hate us, but it never commands us to be friends with our enemies.

"But I say unto you which hear, love your enemies, do good to them which hate you, bless them that curse you, and pray for them which despitefully use you." (Luke 6:27-28 - KJV).

Life itself is like a war zone; you must be alert to the schemes, darts or stray bullets that may be hurled at you. People will hurt you; anyone will hurt you, and you can do likewise. Things happen; life happens, even when you are vigilant. The Bible instructs us to put on the whole armor of God so that we may be able to stand against the wiles of the devil (see Ephesians 6:11). The enemy is a deceiver; he never creates anything but deception. He knows what good plans God has for you here on earth and for eternity, and he does not want you to receive what is rightfully yours that he no longer has access to. As a result, he made it his point of duty to ensure that you do not hear the Word of God. The Word of God is life and light, so you will be able to see and live in your divine purpose.

Apostle Paul wrote to his spiritual son and fellow worker of the gospel to be aware: *"For the time will come when they will not endure sound doctrine; but after their own lusts shall they heap to themselves teachers, having itching ears; and they shall turn away their ears from the truth, and shall be turned unto fables." (2 Timothy 4:3-4 - KJV).* People will not be interested in listening to the truth of God's Word, which is righteous and of good moral and ethical standards, but will be more interested in teachers who tell them what they want to hear and make them feel good, justifying the means even though it is wrong.

OVERCOMING THE FIGHT IN THE PRESENCE OF GOD

In the presence of God, there is safety, protection, provision, and peace guaranteed.

God is a Spirit, and they that worship Him must worship Him in spirit and in truth.

God is omnipresent; He is everywhere all at once. Wherever in the world you are, or whatever time you are reading this book, the presence of the Lord is right there with you. The Holy Spirit is the One who inspired and empowered me to author this book just for you. I needed a tool, a powerhouse like "She Fights," to help me during my dark season. You cannot see Him, not even with a microscope. He is invisible, like the wind. So, you are unable to physically see or touch Him, but you can feel Him deep in your soul. You cannot see or touch the wind, but you can feel it and see the effect of it blowing the leaves, the hem of your dress, or your hair. I hope you get the gist of what I am saying. To be in the presence of God requires a particular posture where your heart and mind are fixed on Him in total reverence. When your heart and mind are in the right posture, your body will conform to the holiness and righteousness of God.

Because God is the Holy Spirit, for you to relate to Him, you need to have faith. Faith is the spiritual vehicle through which you transport your belief to connect with God. This faith is referred to as the substance of things hoped for, the evidence of things not seen (see Hebrews 11:1). Even though you are not able to physically see things, you have a firm belief that it is possible because God has promised it.

Let me ask you: When you sit in a plane, car, train, or whatever mode of transportation, have you ever asked to check the engine to ensure it is in good working condition? Or can you simply accept their word for it and trust that, since they are in operation, it is safe to take you to your destination, so you can confidently sit and enjoy the ride? This is the same way you need to trust God and believe that He is capable, willing, and able to do what He says He will do. God is sovereign; He is omniscient, omnipresent, and omnipotent. He knows all things, and there is nothing hidden from Him. He meant every Word He said, and He is not a man that He should lie (see Numbers 23:19).

I heard the story of two men, namely Mr. Knife and Mr. Fork, having a conversation about the existence of God and the Holy Spirit. One person, Knife, shared his testimony about how God provided for and protected him from accidents, affirming that God is good and faithful. But the other person, Fork, said he did not believe in God because he did not believe God was real. Mr. Knife asked Mr. Fork why he didn't believe in God. Fork replied, *"Because He is not real. I cannot see or touch him."* Knife asked Fork if he had ever experienced excruciating pain. Mr. Fork quickly responded yes. Knife asked him why he should believe that he experienced pain.

Fork said, "It was the worst pain I ever felt in my life, and I will not forget it."

Knife asked Fork, "Can you see the pain?"

Fork answered, "No."

"Can you touch the pain?"

"No," Fork answers.

"So, why should I believe you that you had experienced pain?"

"Because the pain was so excruciating, I thought I was going to lose his mind."

Mr. Knife replied, "Okay, that is the exact way I felt the Holy Spirit moving deep down in my soul, just like how you felt the excruciating pain in your jaw."

The Holy Spirit is real. You cannot see Him or touch Him, but you can feel Him in the core of your being. He is not a figment of our imagination; He is a real spiritual encounter.

To be in the presence of God, you fight the good fight of faith from a place of victory. This battle is not ours; it is the Lord's. This warfare is a spiritual battle; it is like the wind, which you can't see or touch. Flesh cannot fight spirit. You are body, soul, and spirit, so you need to activate the spiritual part of yourself by connecting to God through the Holy Spirit, which is achieved through faith. As you align and apply yourself to God's will, you will overcome.

Be intentional about spending time in the presence of the Lord, where you can have meaningful communication. Isaiah 1:18 says, *"Come, let us reason together,"* which is the Lord God's invitation to dialogue and settle any dispute. He said, *"Though your sins are like scarlet, they shall be as white as snow; though they are red like crimson, they shall become like wool."* What an awesome God!

Spend time with God, meditating on the deep desires of your heart —those unfulfilled dreams and the things you hope for. Ask the Lord to teach you how to pray, and as you read the scriptures, ask the Holy Spirit to give you the revelation to interpret the Word of God for edification and blessings. Ask the Lord what is His plan and purpose for your life, and find out the reason for your why.

You need to know the mind of God as it relates to your life, family, business, ministry, and the world around you. When you spend time in the presence of the Lord, you will be empowered to do greater things and exploits to advance the kingdom of God. Have conversations with God from a place of honesty and openness, without fear and guilt. Approaching God with a grateful heart is not only a delight but a spiritual act of obedience. God has instructed you to give thanks for everything (see 1 Thessalonians 5:18). When you give God thanks, regardless of how you feel, God will give you joy, even in the most challenging situations. Thankfulness opens your heart to the presence of the Lord and your mind to His thoughts, even though the circumstances remain the same.

There may be times when you are so overwhelmed with sorrow and grief that it is almost impossible to be thankful. I implore you to cultivate an attitude of gratitude. A grateful attitude makes it easier to communicate with God and pray without ceasing. Thankfulness will take the sting out of your adversities and give you a clearer view of the Lord's blessings. The more you thank God, the less you will complain and worry. The Bible says we are to cast all our cares on the Lord because He cares for us (see 1 Peter 5:7). So, delight in the Lord, and when your ways please God, He will give you the desires of your heart (see Psalm 37:4).

Surrender your heart and mind to be led by the Holy Spirit because He knows the direction you need to go since He had planned it and has been there before. Since the fall of man in the Garden of Eden, when man sinned against God and hid from the presence of God, and has been hiding ever since, God knows man cannot survive without His presence. So, God has always been seeking to have communication and a relationship with man because that was the purpose for creating man. The only time man has peace is in the presence of God. David said, *"In the presence of the Lord there is fulness of joy, and at His right hand there are pleasures for evermore."* (see Psalm 16:11).

Being in the presence of the Lord will give you hope. You thought you had done things you are ashamed of, but you are not too far gone where the blood of Jesus cannot reach. If you repent and confess to the Lord, He will forgive and cleanse you from all unrighteousness. God also wants you to forgive those who have despitefully used, abused, and refused you so that your heavenly Father will forgive you too.

In the presence of God, there is protection from things seen like rebellion, actions of wicked people and unseen evil thoughts, witchcraft, obeah, necromancy, witches, and warlocks.

"For we wrestle not against flesh and blood, but against principalities, against powers, against the rulers of the darkness of this world, against spiritual wickedness in high places." (Ephesians 6:12 - KJV).

So, just like the children of Israel were told to apply the blood of the sacrificed Lamb, which represented Christ, on the doorpost to protect them from the wrath of God's judgment (see Exodus 12:22-23), you too need the blood of Jesus to protect you so you will be safe from the enemy.

Cavaline Colquhoun

John reminded us, *"And they overcame him by the blood of the Lamb, and by the word of their testimony; and they loved not their lives unto the death." (Revelation 12:11 - KJV)*. To overcome this fight, you must be intentional and be willing to do what is required by staying in the presence of Almighty God, and allowing the Holy Spirit to saturate your mind, body, and soul.

Apostle Paul asked, *"Who shall separate us from the love of Christ? Shall tribulation, or distress, or persecution, or famine, or nakedness, or peril, or sword? As it is written, "For the sake of Christ we are killed all day long, we are accounted as sheep for the slaughter.""* *(Romans 8:35-36 - NKJV)*. He went on to say, *"Yet in all these things we are more than conquerors through Christ who loved us." (Romans 8:37 - NKJV)*.

Make that conscious decision to live for Jesus, no matter what happens. Will it be easy? My answer is a resounding "no," but it is worth every pain. You may have been fighting all your life and were unable to accomplish the goal you yearned for; it was difficult and hurtful, yet you managed through the struggles, the pain, and the tears. You will still fight, but now you will fight in the presence of God, where you can rely on Him.

The Lord is the Spirit and where the Spirit of the Lord is there is liberty. (2 Corinthians 3:17 - NKJV).

Through God we will do valiantly, for it is He who shall tread down our enemies. (Psalm 108:13 - NKJV).

CHAPTER 2

Why Should I Pursue Wisdom?

1. What is Biblical Wisdom?
2. Discipline in Wisdom
3. Developing the Right Skillset

CHAPTER 2 SUMMARY

The fear of the Lord is the beginning of wisdom (see Proverbs 9:10). It is to reverence God for who He is and the authority, wisdom, and power He possesses.

To understand and recognize God's perspective and standard for His people.

To have a deeper insight and connection with God, to know His will and plan for you, and how to apply that wisdom to your life, ministry, and business.

Cavaline Colquhoun

BIBLICAL WISDOM

You may ask, "What is wisdom? Where does wisdom come from?"

Job 28:12-28 gives a clear answer: *"But where shall wisdom be found? and where is the place of understanding? Man knoweth not the price thereof; neither is it found in the land of the living. The depth saith, It is not in me: and the sea saith, It is not with me. It cannot be gotten for gold, neither shall silver be weighed for the price thereof. It cannot be valued with the gold of Ophir, with the precious onyx, or the sapphire. The gold and the crystal cannot equal it: and the exchange of it shall not be for jewels of fine gold. No mention shall be made of coral, or of pearls: for the price of wisdom is above rubies. The topaz of Ethiopia shall not equal it, neither shall it be valued with pure gold. Whence then cometh wisdom? and where is the place of understanding? Seeing it is hid from the eyes of all living, and kept close from the fowls of the air. Destruction and death say, We have heard the fame thereof with our ears. God understandeth the way thereof, and he knoweth the place thereof. For he looketh to the ends of the earth, and seeth under the whole heaven; To make the weight for the winds; and he weigheth the waters by measure. When he made a decree for the rain, and a way for the lightning of the thunder: Then did he see it, and declare it; he prepared it, yea, and searched it out. And unto man he said, Behold, the fear of the Lord, that is wisdom; and to depart from evil is understanding." (KJV).*

God said, *"The fear of the Lord is wisdom and to shun evil is understanding" (Job 28:28 – NIV)*. Wisdom is to revere God for who He is and the authority, wisdom, and power He has. To know wisdom is to know the Word of God. The Word of God is the Living Word that was mentioned in John 1:1, *"In the beginning was the Word, and the Word was with God, and the Word was God." (KJV)*. The Word is a Person, and His name is Jesus Christ.

The Greek word for "Word" is Logos—speech, the divine mind of God—the ultimate truth and guidance of God. *Sanctify them by Your truth. Your word is truth. (John 17:17 - NKJV)*.

The scriptures (Holy Bible) are the breathed Word of God, written by inspired men of God. To know wisdom is to read the Word of God, understand it, and ask the Holy Spirit to reveal the meaning of the scriptures. Take all the information you have gathered through knowledge and experience, and use it to guide you in making good choices that are profitable, productive, and glorify God.

"By the word of the Lord were the heavens made; and all the host of them by the breath of his mouth. He gathereth the waters of the sea together as an heap: he layeth up the depth in storehouses. Let all the earth fear the Lord: let all the inhabitants of the world stand in awe of him. For he spake, and it was done; he commanded, and it stood fast." (Psalm 33:6-9 - KJV).

The Living Word was inscribed on stone, which is the "Ten Commandments," a set of ethical guidelines for relating to God and one another. The apostle Paul admonished his mentee Timothy to obey the Word of God. He explained that *"All scripture is given by inspiration of God, and is profitable for doctrine, for reproof, for correction, for instruction in righteousness: That the man of God may be perfect, thoroughly furnished unto all good works." (2 Timothy 3:16-17 - KJV)*.

President Franklin Delano Roosevelt was the 32nd president of the United States of America. He was the longest-serving US president, serving four terms from 1933 until his death in 1945. FDR, as they called him, encouraged World War II soldiers to read the Bible by printing a letter in the Bibles given to troops before they left for war. The letter began, *"To the members of the Army: As Commander-in-chief, I take pleasure in commending the reading of the Bible to all who serve in the armed forces of the United States."* (Babe, R 1942).

Biblical wisdom enables us to view the world from God's perspective. It helps us understand and recognize God's standpoint and standards for His people, fostering a deeper awareness and connection with God to discern His will and plan for us and how to apply that wisdom to our relationships, ministry, and business.

"If any of you lack wisdom, let him ask of God, that giveth to all men liberally, and upbraideth not; and it shall be given him." (James 1:5 - KJV).

Actively pursue and strive to gain wisdom, as it is not something that is automatically given or readily available; it requires deliberate effort through learning, experience, reflection, and often seeking guidance from others to develop the ability to make sound judgments and navigate life's complexities effectively.

Pursuing wisdom helps you make wiser choices by weighing the pros and cons, the benefits, profits, and the greater good of the majority. It helps to conserve time and energy, reduce loss and waste, and minimize harm and danger.

Wisdom enables you to cultivate positive and meaningful relationships with God and those around you. It helps you maintain a positive mindset, allowing you to see the best in others and situations, and gives you a calm demeanor. It helps you exercise patience, be slow to anger, and be quick to forgive. Wisdom will help you to not only see things for what they are worth but to understand that things are not always as they seem. Biblical wisdom will not only help you do what is expected of you but also do more than what is required if the need arises. At times, it may take you out of your comfort zone and stretch beyond your wildest imagination to extend a hand and a heart of compassion to help someone along the way because this is what Jesus requires of you. If you apply Godly wisdom, you will be able to live a more productive life in gainful employment, a profitable business, a growing ministry, raising a family, and balancing to some degree, regardless of your career.

There is an example found in Genesis 30 that shows if you apply wisdom, God will favour you, increase your produce, and give you wealth.

Jacob had served his father-in-law, Laban, for twenty years, of which fourteen were spent marrying his two daughters, Rachel and Leah, as a bride price—and six years tending to his flock. Soon after Rachel had given birth to Joseph, Jacob went to Laban and asked him to release him so he could return home to his own country. Jacob requested to take his wives and children, for he had earned them by serving Laban. *"I have become wealthy, for the Lord has blessed me because of you." (Genesis 30:27 - NLT).* So, he asked Jacob how much he owed him, and whatever it was, he would pay. Jacob replied, *"You know how hard I've worked for you, and how your flocks and herds have grown under my care. You had little indeed before I came, but your wealth has increased enormously. The Lord has blessed you through everything I've done. But now, what about me? When can I start providing for my own family?" (Genesis 30:29-30 - NLT).*

Laban ignored Jacob's wish and asked him how much he would like to be paid. Jacob replied, *"Don't give me anything. Just do this one thing, and I'll continue to tend and watch over your flocks. Let me inspect your flocks today and remove all the sheep and goats that are speckled or spotted, along with all the black sheep. Give these to me as my wages. In the future, when you check on the animals you have given me as my wages, you'll see that I have been honest. If you find in my flock any goats without speckles or spots, or any sheep that are not black, you will know that I have stolen them from you."* Laban agreed and replied, *"It will be as you say."*

The same day, Laban went out and removed the male goats that were streaked and spotted, all the female goats that were speckled and spotted or had white patches, and all the black sheep. He placed them in the care of his own sons, who took them a three-day journey, approximately 75–90 miles from where Jacob was. Meanwhile, Jacob stayed and cared for the rest of Laban's flock.

God gave Jacob the wisdom to use some fresh branches from poplar, almond, and plane trees and peeled off strips of bark, making white streaks on them. Then he placed the peeled branches in the watering troughs where the flocks would come to drink, for that was where they mated. And when they mated in front of the white-streaked branches, they gave birth to young that were streaked, speckled and spotted. This was how Jacob built his own flock instead of increasing Laban's. As a result, Jacob became very wealthy, with large flocks of sheep and goats, female and male servants, and many camels and donkeys. (see Genesis 30:35-40).

If you need wisdom, pray and ask God. He is the Omniscient God, knowing all things. He said, *"If you need wisdom, ask, and He will give it to you liberally." (James 1:5 - NKJV).* Jesus said in Matthew 7:7-8, *"Ask, and it shall be given you; seek, and ye shall find; knock, and it shall be opened unto you: For every one that asketh receiveth; and he that seeketh findeth; and to him that knocketh it shall be opened." (KJV).*

Godly wisdom will help you walk in God's divine will. Look at King Solomon, who was crowned when he was just a teenager. He realized that he was inexperienced and didn't know how to lead the people. So, he asked God to give him wisdom, and God granted him far more than he had anticipated. He wasn't only the wisest man who ever lived, but he was also blessed with wealth and honor (see 1 Kings 3:12-13).

Of all the wisdom, wealth, honour, and luxury Solomon had, that never stopped him from falling into temptation. Solomon forgot the instructions and promises God gave him, disobeyed God, married foreign women, built temples, and worshiped idols. Solomon had everything to his heart's content, yet the lust of the flesh, the lust of the eyes, and the pride of life set in (see 1 John 2:16).

Solomon learned his lessons and gave wise counsel to his children.

"Trust in the Lord with all thine heart; and lean not unto thine own understanding. In all thy ways acknowledge him,

and he shall direct thy paths. Be not wise in thine own eyes: fear the Lord, and depart from evil." (Proverbs 3:5-7 - KJV).

When Solomon examined his life, he concluded that all is vanity; all is meaningless.

"I have seen all the works that are done under the sun; and behold, all is vanity and vexation of spirit. That which is crooked cannot be made straight: and that which is wanting cannot be numbered. I communicated with mine own heart, saying, Lo, I have come to great estate, and have gotten more wisdom than all that has been before me in Jerusalem: yea, my heart had great experience of wisdom and knowledge. I gave my heart to know wisdom, and to know madness and folly: I perceived that this also is vexation of spirit. For in much wisdom there is much grief and he that increases knowledge increases sorrow." (Ecclesiastes 1:14-18 – KJV).

Solomon's legacy is one of wisdom that can only be useful if applied. Human nature cannot be changed by wisdom alone; it takes Godly wisdom to walk in the purpose of God for your life.

Let us hear the conclusion of the whole matter: Fear God and keep his commandments: for this is the whole duty of man. For God shall bring every work into judgment, with every secret thing, whether it be good, or whether it be evil. (Ecclesiastes 12:13-14 – NKJV).

Cavaline Colquhoun

Paul says we should not look at the troubles we can see now; rather, fix our gaze on things that cannot be seen (see 2 Corinthians 4:18). For the things we see now will soon be gone, but the things we cannot see will last forever.

Set your affection on things above, not on things on the earth. Let the word of Christ dwell in you richly in all wisdom; teaching and admonishing one another in psalms and hymns and spiritual songs, singing with grace in your hearts to the Lord. (Colossians 3:2, 16 - KJV).

Biblical wisdom will help you focus on what is truly important and live a Christ-centered life. As 2 Timothy 2:12 states, *"If we suffer, we shall also reign with him: if we deny him, he also will deny us:"* Jesus is coming back for His bride. He wants you adorned, ready, and waiting for His appearance. Nothing is worth your soul; there will be no excuses for wealth, job, business, relationship, or who wronged you. Guilt and regrets will not be accepted.

But the day of the Lord will come as unexpectedly as a thief. Then the heavens will pass away with a terrible noise, and the very elements themselves will disappear in fire, and the earth and everything on it will be found to deserve judgment. Since everything around us is going to be destroyed like this, what holy and godly lives you should live, looking forward to the day of God and hurrying it along. On that day, he will set the heavens on fire, and the elements will melt away in the flames. (2 Peter 3:10-12 - NLT).

DISCIPLINE IN WISDOM

From the beginning, holiness has been the norm for human nature, being created in the image of God, and God said it was good. The day Adam disobeyed God, sin entered the world. Since then, we all have sinned and fallen short of the glory of God. Sin is considered a foreign element and is not a normal part of human nature. It's rebellion, a violation of sovereignty and a perfect universe. Sin involves all aspects of personal nature, including the mind, emotion, and will—where the mind substitutes a lie for truth, the heart hatred for love, and the will substitutes the subjection of one's own will for the subjection to God.

Discipline is the ability to control oneself and work consistently in a structured manner by following established rules or standards. It helps to correct and mold the mental faculty or moral character. Discipleship has an aim in view; it comes with a price, and it will cost you a lot, depending on what you hope to achieve.

This approach requires consistency, commitment, and a deliberate effort on the part of the individual to accomplish a goal. Discipline is goal-oriented, with its agenda focused on the prize.

1 Peter 1:13 states that we are to gird/guard the loins of our minds. Prepare your mind for whatever lies ahead; be ready for the challenges, and do not be easily distracted but focus on the goal.

Apart from Jesus Christ, Solomon was said to be the wisest man who ever lived. Solomon was only a teen when he was crowned king.

One night, Solomon had a dream in which he and the Lord had a conversation, during which the Lord asked him what he would like Him to give him. The young king answered, *"Lord, give me an understanding heart to judge Your people that I may discern between good and evil."* Solomon didn't ask for long life or riches, nor did he ask to take the life of his enemies. So, God gave Solomon wisdom unlike any other before or after him. And God also gave Solomon riches and honour that he never asked for as added blessings. God also promised him that he would lengthen his life if he walked in God's way and obeyed God's statutes and commandments, just as his father David had done (see 1 Kings 3:5-15).

King Solomon was the one who built the temple.

Wisdom will teach you what to listen to and who to listen to. Discipline in wisdom is achieved through the power of the Holy Spirit. He will teach you how to apply different strategies, when to rebuke the enemy (the devil), and when to stand still. Shun the very appearance of the devil; that is, anything that looks like the enemy, such as craftiness, undermining, etc.

Wisdom will teach you how to pray. Instead of asking God for the things you think you need, ask God to teach you how to pray. Pray for God's will to be done; that whatever He has planned for you will be realized.

"For gaining wisdom and instruction; for understanding words of insight; for receiving instruction in prudent behavior, doing what is right and just and fair." (Proverbs 1:2-3 – NIV).

"Whoever heeds discipline shows the way to life, but whoever ignores correction leads others astray." (Proverbs 10:17 – NIV).

"Whoever loves discipline loves knowledge, but he who hates reproof is stupid." (Proverbs 12:1 – EST).

Wisdom is to understand the mind of God. Knowing the mind of God is very important because it allows individuals to understand God's perspective, purpose, and values for their life. It will guide their actions, decisions, and overall outlook on life. Maintaining a relationship with God enables us to live with wisdom and care for one another, reflecting Christlikeness.

"He that hath no rule over his own spirit is like a city that is broken down, and without walls." (Proverbs 25:28 - KJV).

"I discipline my body like an athlete, training it to do what it should. Otherwise, I fear that after preaching to others I myself might be disqualified." (1 Corinthians 9:27 – NLT).

Cavaline Colquhoun

DEVELOPING THE RIGHT SKILL-SET

Everyone was created for God's purpose. God gave everyone gifts and talents to carry out specific responsibilities that He would have them fulfill for His purpose, regardless of their abilities and availabilities. You should value what He has deposited in you, cherish and nurture what you have, and not neglect or bury them but practice refining your art in serving your master. While some talents are innate, others can be learned and skillfully developed through consistent practice and effort to be effective in ministry and business.

Your goal may not be your purpose, but your purpose should definitely be your goal.

God wants you to use what He has given you to serve others, to advance His kingdom, and to glorify His name. For example, God gave you two eyes, but you cannot see yourself; others would have to tell you what you look like unless you look in a mirror. You cannot see yourself; you must depend on others to tell you about yourself. Likewise, you can see others and tell them about themselves. That is why the Bible says that we need each other to survive. We are all servants of the living God, and so, the talents He has given you are not for your personal use or to add to your resume but to equip you to serve others.

As Apostle Peter says in 1 Peter 4:10-11, *"Each one has received a special gift; employ it in serving one another as good stewards of the multifaceted grace of God." Whoever speaks is to do so as one who is speaking actual words of God; whoever serves is to do so as one who is serving by the strength which God supplies; so that in all things God may be glorified through Jesus Christ, to whom belongs the glory and dominion forever and ever. Amen." (AMP).*

Whatever you do, work from the heart. Put in your very best effort as for the Lord and not for people, knowing that it is from the Lord that you will receive the reward of inheritance (legacy). You serve the Lord Jesus Christ (see Colossians 3:23-24).

As a coach, regardless of how I feel, I must prepare my lesson (PowerPoint, question-and-answer, fill-in-the-blank, or assigning tasks)—whatever I may be using to teach. Whether I am hurting or not, I am obligated and expected to deliver well. I recall that at the end of a session, I would often tumble over and cry out to God for physical and spiritual strength. This is not playing hypocrite, but I have a task to carry out. People are not interested in your excuses, though they may be legitimate. They pay for a service, and you made them a promise. They are expected to receive their product to solve or resolve a need, and excuses will not suffice. It may sound harsh, but it's reality. It is called business or ministry.

Everyone should make a plan, whether for school, career, professional development, relationships, business, ministry, or vacation. Whatever you hope to do or become, you need to map out a plan, a blueprint, or something that will give you a sense of direction. If God had a plan and He is omniscient, we too should have goals. God spoke to the prophet Jeremiah, saying, *"I know the plan I have for you, a plan of peace and not of evil, to give you a future and a hope." (Jeremiah 29:11 – NIV).* God wants you to know that He has a plan for you, even before you were created. Every day of your life was carefully thought through, so as you plan with God in mind, He will establish it (see Proverbs 16:3).

You may have a plan, but it may not be working in your favour or productive. Or you may not have a plan at all. You may no longer know exactly what you want to do, probably because you have tried so many times and it doesn't seem possible anymore. You may think that time has elapsed too many times, and age may become a factor, or you may not have the resources to accomplish your dreams. However, I guarantee that if you start today, in six months' time, you will be six months ahead in business, school, or ministry.

If you don't have any skills or need to develop your skills, ask yourself these three questions and take some time to think about them and answer honestly:

1. What am I great at?
2. What am I good at?
3. What am I weak at?

What you are great at is something you may love, understand, and naturally gravitate towards. This may require less effort to accomplish them. Mark Twain said, *"Find a job you enjoy doing, and you will never have to work a day in your life."* Regardless of your job description, if it aligns with your purpose and passion, you may enjoy the tasks so much that it feels like achieving a goal or fulfilling a dream. It's equally important to identify what you're good at so you can improve your skills with confidence and dexterity. Then, you will be able to impact and influence those you serve with what you know, your knowledge, your experiences, and the things you have overcome.

Identifying your weaknesses is actually a strength you should appreciate. This is the first step towards getting the help you need to accomplish what you desire, allowing you to achieve your goals.

Regardless of a good plan, it's the skill that will bring success (see Ecclesiastes 10:10). It's nice to be ambitious and graduate from a prestigious university at the top of your class, with walls filled with accolades. However, you cannot be an expert in a field until you put your craft into practice. This is the only way you will be able to hone your skills when you have done the work and mastered the art. When you are committed and consistent, you will excel at what you do and maximize the impact you have on those around you. After you have mastered your skills, you need to ensure that you remain current as things change over time; what was acceptable today may change somewhat tomorrow.

Developing your skillset requires a collaborative effort, as you will not be able to do it alone. Discipline comes with choices, and with choices comes effort. The effort is by far the most difficult at the beginning. So, it's okay to ask for help: consider getting a mentor, a support system, or an accountability partner who will encourage you and check in regularly to ensure you're staying on track and working towards your goals. Create a structure that works especially well for one-on-one interactions.

CHAPTER 3

Is Wisdom By Choice or By Chance (How to Walk in Wisdom)

1. How to Walk in Wisdom
2. Chance or Choice?
3. The Repercussion of Your Decision

CHAPTER 3 SUMMARY

Wisdom is largely considered a choice rather than a chance.

Wisdom is critical in fighting. It involves consistently acquiring knowledge and applying it to make informed judgments.

Wisdom is a conscious decision of choosing when to act skillfully rather than impulsively reacting to situations.

Wisdom is more powerful than weapons. However, one mistake can destroy everything, and the repercussions can be great.

Cavaline Colquhoun

WALKING IN THE WAY OF WISDOM

At creation, God created everything in the world that man needed before He created man to show us His love through His provision and protection. Then, there was a turn-away where man no longer desired the things of God but sought pleasure in satisfying and appeasing the flesh. Man was not made for the world, but the world was made for man to glorify God and to love one another.

To walk in the way of wisdom is to walk with God. Life is a one-way street. We will only pass this way but once, and the path on this journey is uncertain. There are dangers lurking all around, and we do not know the way, so we need the Holy Spirit to lead us safely through the terrain and storms. Since we have not been in this position before and will never experience this life again, we must strive to live to the best of our abilities, doing what is right and righteous in the sight of God and humanity. To know how to venture ahead, we need to ask the One who knows the way, the One who designed the blueprint.

Jesus saith unto him, I am the way, the truth, and the life: no man cometh unto the Father, but by me. (John 14:6 – KJV).

Walking with God means knowing and obeying Him by reading His Word, praying and seeking His face, trusting Him, and following where He leads. Like a young child who knows their mother and desires sincere milk and all that they need from their mother, so God wants you to yearn after Him for who He is and for His provision. In so doing, you first need to acknowledge who God is, that He is the Saviour of your soul, the One who came to redeem you from sin, to have a relationship with you, and to take you to the place He has prepared for you.

He wants you to walk the path He has designed for you, even before you were conceived in your mother's womb, because He has a perfect plan that will give you an expected outcome and a positive future (see Jeremiah 29:11), regardless of the trials and opposition you may encounter.

Since the fall, human beings have had the tendency to follow their heart and do what pleases them. They have a natural inclination towards happiness and instant gratification, a desire for more pleasure, and a strong aversion to pain at all costs. Humans are inherently needy, and we are motivated by our needs.

Maslow's hierarchy of needs is a psychological theory that describes humans' needs, categorized into five levels, and each level must be met in a specific order. At the base of the pyramid are physiological needs, which are priority number one, meaning that they must be met before any other needs can be considered. Humans cannot live or exist without them. These include air, food, water, sleep, clothing, shelter, and sex or reproduction. There is a need for safety within and outside the home to feel secure from threats and uncertainties. This is where law and order are enforced and a justice system that serves the welfare of the people. As a relational being, we strive and grow through love. As the first commandment states, we must love the Lord our God and love our neighbor as we love ourselves (see Mark 12:30-31). When we love and care for each other, we will feel accepted and respected, knowing we have the freedom to choose and excel to our greatest potential as human beings.

Walking in the way of wisdom, the Holy Spirit will nudge you to realize that whatever you are doing is not working, and you need to stop it completely. Try something new, change your method, or adjust your strategy to achieve your desired goal. The Holy Spirit will also show you where not to go and what to avoid to reach your destination. There are potential downsides to making decisions without considering how they might negatively impact the needs of others. It may result in a conflict of interest that may jeopardize relationships, business, and ministry.

To travel from point A to point B, you need to have a sense of direction to know how to get there. You may use a map, compass, Waze, signs, or arrows, or ask someone who knows the route. For example, when a pilot has been assigned to take the aircraft to a particular place on a particular route, even if he has never been before, he is expected to carefully follow the heading indicator (HI), also known as a directional gyro (DG), to take him safely to the prescribed destination. He may encounter dark clouds and tremulous winds on route but must stay the course and stay connected. If the pilot chooses to do otherwise, he will endanger himself, and all those on board are at risk of losing their lives. So, regardless of the pilots' knowledge of the destination, there are standard protocols that must be adhered to in order to land safely and in a timely manner.

As drivers, we are expected to adhere to road codes to ensure we reach our destinations safely. However, there are times when some drivers, for some reason, choose to do otherwise, ending in accidents that cause pain, disabilities, and even death. On this journey of life, God wants us to focus on Him, allowing Him to guide us safely through to our final destination. He wants us to focus on Him and not be distracted by the things on the way, for they are only temporal. God wants us to use all that He has entrusted to us and in our care to serve others and advance His kingdom here on earth, and He will reward us with a crown of life in heaven.

I have taught you in the way of wisdom; I have led you in the right paths. When you walk, your steps will not be hindered, and when you run, you will not stumble (Proverbs 4:11-12 - NKJV).

See then that you walk circumspectly, not as fools but as wise, redeeming the time, because the days are evil. (Ephesians 5:15-16 - NKJV).

CHANCE OR CHOICE

Wisdom is considered a choice rather than a chance. It is not a coincidence that the word "WISDOM" is mentioned more than 234 times in the Bible and over 54 times in the book of Proverbs alone. God specifically instructs us to:

"Get wisdom! Get understanding! Do not forget, nor turn away from the words of my mouth. Do not forsake her, and she will preserve you; Love her, and she will keep you. Wisdom is the principal thing; Therefore get wisdom. And in all your getting, get understanding. Exalt her, and she will promote you; She will bring you honor, when you embrace her. She will place on your head an ornament of grace; a crown of glory she will deliver to you." (Proverbs 4:5-9 - NKJV).

Wisdom is a conscious decision to choose when to act skillfully rather than impulsively reacting to situations.

Choose my instruction rather than silver, and knowledge rather than pure gold. For wisdom is far more valuable than rubies. Nothing you desire can compare with it. "I, Wisdom, live together with good judgment. I know where to discover knowledge and discernment. All who fear the Lord will hate evil. Therefore, I hate pride and arrogance, corruption and perverse speech. Common sense and success belong to me. Insight and strength are mine. Because of me, kings reign, and rulers make just decrees. Rulers lead with my help, and nobles make righteous judgments. (Proverbs 8:10-16 - NLT).

Wisdom is not something you simply acquire by chance. You need to actively look for it and work towards understanding it. Actively pursue and strive to gain wisdom, as it is not something automatically given or readily available; it requires deliberate effort through learning, experience, reflection, and often seeking guidance from others to develop the ability to make sound judgments and navigate life's complexities effectively.

See wisdom as your ultimate goal; place it above all material possessions. Once you obtain wisdom, it should be held fast and not given up.

To hold on to wisdom means actively preserving and continually applying the knowledge and understanding you've gained through experience and learning, essentially making it a guiding principle in your life and not letting it slip away. It implies actively seeking to maintain insight and using it to make sound decisions in various situations.

Applying knowledge: True wisdom extends beyond merely acquiring information; it involves utilizing that knowledge to navigate life with sound judgment and make informed, ethical choices.

Intentional effort: It's not passive; you need to consciously choose to reflect on experiences, learn from mistakes, and enthusiastically seek out new perspectives to maintain wisdom.

Continuous learning: Wisdom is a lifelong pursuit, so staying open to new, innovative ideas and experiences is crucial to keep your wisdom relevant. Proverbs 4:6 says, *"Hold on to instruction, do not let go; guard it, for it is your life." (NIV).* Getting wisdom is a lifelong learning experience.

We must be intentional in whatever we say and do, and walking in wisdom should be a matter of choice not chance, because God has instructed us to walk in His wisdom.

"Here is another bit of wisdom that has impressed me as I have watched the way our world works. There was a small town with only a few people, and a great king came with his army and besieged it. A poor, wise man knew how to save the town, and so it was rescued. But afterward no one thought to thank him. So even though wisdom is better than strength, those who are wise will be despised if they are poor. What they say will not be appreciated for long. Better to hear the quiet words of a wise person than the shouts of a foolish king. Better to have wisdom than weapons of war, but one sinner can destroy much that is good." (Ecclesiastes 9:13-18 – NLT).

Knowing the importance of these valuable assets, Solomon encouraged us to buy the truth and not sell it, as well as wisdom, instruction, and understanding (see Proverbs 23:23). Wisdom will guide you in knowing what to do before you act. Running fast in a race does not make you the winner, but running in the right direction and finishing the race does.

For wisdom is better than rubies; and all the things that may be desired are not to be compared to it. I wisdom dwell with prudence, and find out knowledge of witty inventions (Proverbs 8:11-12 - KJV).

Wisdom is worth more than all the money and wealth combined in this world. It cannot be traded; you cannot give anything in exchange for it. You should be willing to make every sacrifice to obtain it. When you have acquired wisdom, you should guard it with your life and teach the next generation.

I will share a story of wise leadership, illustrating how wisdom-related qualities play a crucial role in overcoming leadership challenges and contribute to leaders' outstanding success. Anne Mulcahy is credited with keeping the Xerox Corporation afloat by successfully navigating the financial and ethical challenges the company faced in the early 2000s. Taking over the CEO role, Mulcahy was advised to take the easy route and declare bankruptcy. Taking a bigger-picture perspective, Mulcahy recognized that such a decision could have ruined the company and any long-term prospects for a viable future. She displayed intellectual humility by personally meeting with stakeholders, allowing them to voice their concerns, heeding advice, taking personal responsibility, and apologizing for the company's past mistakes.

She made a firm commitment to ethics, human rights, and sustainable business practices, including rectifying past wrongs in accounting and addressing social irresponsibility. *"By doing the right thing for our stakeholders and the global community,"* she said, *"we're also doing what's right for our business" (Canada).* Mulcahy has been widely recognized and praised for her actions, receiving a CEO of the Year award in 2008. Yet, she humbly defers credit to her colleagues and subordinates, stating that her success *"represents the impressive accomplishments of Xerox people around the world."* It appears that Anne Mulcahy's intellectual humility in the face of complex challenges, as well as her accommodation of different perspectives, needs, and values, all played a significant role during the critical moment, allowing her to harness positive outcomes for both the company and herself. The company remained stable for a few years after Mulcahy's retirement in 2009, fighting an up-fill battle in the post-print digital age. (Canada).

"Choose for yourselves today whom you will serve." (Joshua 24:15 – NKJV).

The enduring significance of Hill's philosophy assures us that success is forged not by chance but through the deliberate cultivation of belief and the pursuit of well-defined goals. Through the steadfast application of this wisdom, individuals unlock their potential, transforming the presumable into the physical.

THE REPERCUSSION OF YOUR DECISIONS

Repercussions are usually considered bad because the impacts normally have a negative connotation to it. The result of actions, events, or failure to act may not be evident immediately and can last for years and generations. Therefore, it is imperative that we carefully consider our actions and words before speaking, as a word, once spoken, cannot be taken back, and some actions can be dangerous and even fatal. From the beginning, God has been giving man clear instructions to obey Him, and those who do will be positively rewarded. Likewise, if they refuse, there will be negative consequences and repercussions, both physical and spiritual.

Some physical repercussions could result from poor choices, unresolved conflict, and trauma that can lead to pain and suffering through sicknesses and diseases. There are also spiritual repercussions resulting from the sin of omission and negative actions, which lead to regret, guilt, remorse, loss of peace, and eternal separation and damnation.

Then the Lord God took the man and put him in the garden of Eden to tend and keep it. And the Lord God commanded the man, saying, "Of every tree of the garden you may freely eat; but of the tree of the knowledge of good and evil you shall not eat, for in the day that you eat of it you shall surely die." (Genesis 2:15-17 – NKJV).

Repercussion is also referred to as backlash or counterattack.

The scripture said that God created Adam and Eve and placed them in the Garden of Eden, and initially, they had a perfect relationship and lived completely in harmony. However, this perfect relationship was severed when man disobeyed God's command and sin entered into the world. This separation from God causes man to feel a sense of guilt, shame, nakedness, or spiritual emptiness.

Now the serpent was more cunning than any beast of the field which the Lord God had made. And he said to the woman, "Has God indeed said, 'You shall not eat of every tree of the garden'?" And the woman said to the serpent, "We may eat the fruit of the trees of the garden; but of the fruit of the tree which is in the midst of the garden, God has said, 'You shall not eat it, nor shall you touch it, lest you die.'" Then the serpent said to the woman, "You will not surely die. For God knows that in the day you eat of it your eyes will be opened, and you will be like God, knowing good and evil." So when the woman saw that the tree was good for food, that it was pleasant to the eyes, and a tree desirable to make one wise, she took of its fruit and ate. She also gave to her husband with her, and he ate. Then the eyes of both of them were opened, and they knew that they were naked; and they sewed fig leaves together and made themselves coverings. (Genesis 3:1-7 - NKJV).

When man sinned, man automatically separated themselves from God, renounced their loyalty and trust, and hid themselves from God, who went after them and covered their shame and nakedness. God so loved us that He gave us His only beloved Son (see John 3:16) to die on the cross and rose again as a sacrifice, which acts as a means of reconciliation, allowing humans to be forgiven for their sins and re-establish a connection with God through faith and acceptance of Jesus as their Lord and Saviour (see Colossians 1:19-22).

"For I will be merciful toward their iniquities, and I will remember their sins no more." (Hebrews 8:12 – ESV).

"Beloved, let us cleanse ourselves from all defilement of flesh and spirit, perfecting holiness in the fear of God." (2 Corinthians 7:1 – NASB).

"Be not deceived; God is not mocked: for whatsoever a man soweth, that shall he also reap." (Galatians 6:7 - KJV).

If you plant red beans, red beans will grow, and red beans are what you will reap at harvest time. You should not expect to reap white beans when you did not plant white beans. Do not deceive yourself into believing that you can plant one thing and reap something totally different. Don't take the Lord for a fool.

"For every action, there is an equal and opposite reaction." —Isaac Newton

Cavaline Colquhoun

In the 1600s, Sir Isaac Newton, an English polymath known as a walking encyclopedia, was active as a mathematician, physicist, astronomer, alchemist, theologian, and author, as well as a natural philosopher. He invented the third law of motion, which stated that every action has an equal and opposite reaction. He explained that if you press a button with your finger, your finger is also pressed by that button. Every action, whether big or small, good or bad, visible or invisible, leads to a result, whether favorable or not.

The consequences of our actions can be positive or negative; for example, staying up late can result in being tired and grumpy the next day. If you help someone in need, you might feel good about yourself. If you refuse to assist someone when you could, you may feel guilty and have a sense of remorse. An act of unprofessionalism on the job can lead to suspension or permanent dismissal. Understanding how consequences influence behavior is a key element in changing one's behavior. We reward positive behaviour and punish those behaviours that are considered unacceptable; either way, they can strengthen the association between actions and their consequences.

It is crucial for us to make responsible choices and be conscious of the decisions we make, accepting full responsibility for the outcomes. You need to consider how your actions, or the lack thereof, impact others and how you perceive or misinterpret situations correctly.

CHAPTER 4

How Much Are You Worth?

1. Created in the Image of Royalty
2. Robed In Righteousness
3. Qualified Without Title

CHAPTER 4 SUMMARY

The Bible said when God created you, He said it was good. You are the apple of His eyes. You are fearfully and wonderfully made.

You are priceless, with inherent worth and value, because God has placed that value on you.

The fact that God could give up His one and only Son to die for your sin and to take your shame and guilt just shows the measure of His unconditional love. That speaks volumes of your worth.

I am crucified with Christ: nevertheless I live; yet not I, but Christ liveth in me: and the life which I now live in the flesh

Cavaline Colquhoun

I live by the faith of the Son of God, who loved me, and gave himself for me. (Galatians 2:20 - KJV).

For this cause we also, since the day we heard it, do not cease to pray for you, and to desire that ye might be filled with the knowledge of his will in all wisdom and spiritual understanding; That ye might walk worthy of the Lord unto all pleasing, being fruitful in every good work, and increasing in the knowledge of God; (Colossians 1:9-10).

Being born again, not of corruptible seed, but of incorruptible, by the word of God, which liveth and abideth for ever. (1 Peter 1:23 - KJV).

Therefore if any man be in Christ, he is a new creature: old things are passed away; behold, all things are become new. (2 Corinthians 5:17 - KJV).

I am an ambassador for Christ (see 2 Corinthians 5:20). I am part of a chosen generation, a royal priesthood, a holy nation, a purchased people (see 1 Peter 2:9).

I am a joint heir with Christ (see Romans 8:17). I am more than a conqueror through Him who loves me (see Romans 8:37).

The wise woman builds her house by raising children, working diligently, and being successful in ministry and business, along with all she sets out to accomplish. In contrast, other women destroy their homes by neglecting their families (see Proverbs 14:1).

House and riches are the inheritance of fathers: and a prudent wife is from the Lord. (Proverbs 19:14 – KJV).

If you had asked God for something and have not received it yet, it is likely that the Lord is either saying, "Wait," "Not yet," or "No." Accept whatever answer you may have gotten from the Lord. *How do you know that was the answer from the Lord and not your mind playing tricks on you?* Try the spirit by aligning it with the Word of God.

If God says "wait," then God is preparing you for whatever you have asked for according to His divine will and purpose. God always has something far better and bigger than what we may hope or ask for. Because you are not omniscient and cannot see the whole picture, God allows you to wait until you can appreciate the full package He has in store for you. God knows exactly what we need when we need it, though scary it may be. He wants you to take Him at His word and wait on Him, for His timing is perfect.

God's perfect timing is critical in walking in your worth when we place our lives in His hands and ask Him to lead and direct our paths in the way we should go, according to His perfect will. God wants you to trust Him regardless of what may be happening around you. Be patient.

David waited fifteen years; Joseph waited twenty-two years; Moses waited forty years. Wait patiently for the Lord. Be brave and courageous. Yes, wait patiently for the Lord (see Psalm 27:14). I don't know how long you might be waiting but if the Lord says wait, WAIT ON GOD

"I will answer them before they even call to me. While they are still talking about their needs, I will go ahead and answer their prayers." (Isaiah 65:24 - NLT).

God is reminding you that He is near, He is with you wherever you are and He not only knows your needs but had already made provision to meet those needs in His perfect timing.

For you created my inmost being; you knit me together in my mother's womb. I praise you because I am fearfully and wonderfully made; your works are wonderful, I know that full well. My frame was not hidden from you when I was made in the secret place, when I was woven together in the depths of the earth. Your eyes saw my unformed body; all the days ordained for me were written in your book before one of them came to be. (Psalm 139:13-16 - NIV).

"Before I formed you in the womb I knew you, before you were born, I set you apart." (Jeremiah 1:5 - NIV).

And this same God who takes care of me will supply all your needs from his glorious riches, which have been given to us in Christ Jesus. (Philippians 4:19 - NLT).

I love fine cars, and Lexus is one of my favorites. I was told that if anything goes wrong, I must take it back to the Lexus car dealer, who has specialist mechanics for that specific make and model. Why? Because they are the ones who made it. They know how to repair and already have the parts needed. So, likewise, God who created us knows us more than we know ourselves. He knows our needs, desires, likes and dislikes and has the resources to meet them.

Look at the lilies and how they grow. They don't work or make their clothing, yet Solomon in all his glory was not dressed as beautifully as they are. And if God cares so wonderfully for flowers that are here today and thrown into the fire tomorrow, he will certainly care for you. Why do you have so little faith? (Luke 12:27-28 - NLT).

CREATED IN THE IMAGE OF ROYALTY

Humans are created in the image and likeness of God, who is considered the ultimate Ruler and King, giving man a special status and responsibility to act as stewards and representatives of God on earth, essentially acting as "royalty" in their own right; this concept originates from Genesis: *"Let us make man in our image, after our likeness." (Genesis 1:26 - KJV).* Royalty suggests that humans share certain characteristics with God, such as the ability to reason, love, and make moral choices. We have spiritual authority, power, and the ability to reflect God's standard of living, like holiness and righteousness, and to be a good steward of what the Lord has entrusted in our care.

Cavaline Colquhoun

Created in the image of royalty reminds me of the song "She's Royal." Royalty denotes power and prestige. The image of royalty is not so much the superficial glitz and glamour of material wealth, but it is for us to delve deep on a spiritual level that we are indeed created in the image and likeness of God, the Creator of all things, in the heavens, on earth, and under the earth (see Genesis 1).

Made for royalty means something is of such high quality, elegance, and luxury that it is considered suitable for a king or queen. It is usually designed with the finest materials, including expensive fabrics and precious metals, and features craftsmanship for the most privileged and astute individuals in society. Products are not mass-produced and are not commonly found in marketplaces but are custom-built with intricate designs befitting the status of royalty.

To be born into royalty suggests that you are born into a royal family, which would make you a princess or a king's child, and you will one day inherit the throne of God. To be royal is to be a diplomat.

A diplomat is a person whose job is to maintain relationships between the governments of different countries—someone who lives in a foreign country and works to understand the needs and concerns of other countries. They strive to guide countries toward mutually agreeable decisions, protect their citizens, repair relationships between nations, foster lasting bonds that shape foreign policy, and maintain political, economic, and social relations with other countries.

Diplomatic immunity is a status granted to diplomats that exempts them from the laws of the foreign jurisdiction in which they are serving.

Diplomats receive a variety of benefits, including:

- **Allowances and incentives:** These can include foreign travel per diem allowances, cost of living allowances, and recruitment and retention incentives.

- **Housing:** Diplomats may receive free housing or other housing allowances.

- **Travel:** Diplomats often travel extensively, providing a valuable opportunity to interact with people from diverse cultures.

- **Immunities:** Diplomats are protected by diplomatic immunity, which exempts them from local jurisdiction, allowing them to perform their duties freely.

- **Health benefits:** Diplomats may receive health benefit plans, life insurance, and long-term care insurance.

- **Leave:** Diplomats may receive annual leave, paid holidays, and sick leave.

- **Family-friendly benefits:** Diplomats may receive childcare subsidies, a childcare center, and family medical leave.

- **Other benefits include** access to a credit union, fitness facility, employee consultation service, and employee recreation association.

- **Networking:** Diplomats have the opportunity to network with people from around the world.

- **Training:** Diplomats may receive training through classes, programs, and mentoring.

A diplomat's status typically lasts for the duration of their posting to a foreign country, which is usually between two and four years, but can be extended depending on the assignment and the discretion of the sending government. They can be recalled at any time by the State Department.

As children of God, we are created in royalty; we are citizens of the kingdom. We are ambassadors for Christ, representing the kingdom of God here on earth (see 2 Corinthians 5:20). We are diplomats in this world, on God's assignment to rebuild strained relationships, promote peace and harmony, and care for the needs of people. We spread His message of love and grace through our actions and words, effectively serving as a bridge between God and the world. We demonstrate God's goodness and truth to others through our daily lives and actively promote reconciliation with God through the message of the gospel.

ROBED IN RIGHTEOUSNESS

A robe is a loose-fitting outer garment that covers the body for warmth, complement, and protection. It also symbolizes different things to different people and cultures. For example, a symbol of cultural tradition, a robe is often given as a gesture of hospitality. Robes often signify wealth, status, and authority (see Luke 7:25, Matthew 11:8). Those robes, regardless of the color, style, or symbols displayed, are an outer garment and not a true reflection of the human heart; they are temporal, superficial, and are only a product of human effort. On a sad note, though, robes were also used to convey false honour and mockery as was ascribed during the passion of Jesus when He was stripped of His clothes and was clothed in a scarlet and purple robe to mock Him (see Matthew 27:28 and John 19:5) as King of the Jews, not realizing He is the King of all kings and the Lord of lords (see Revelation 17:14).

There are robes that symbolize forgiveness, restoration, and acceptance back into the family, as seen in the parable told by Jesus about the prodigal son who asked for his inheritance and left his home to go to a foreign country. He wasted all on riotous living, and when he came to his senses, he went back home. However, his father was always looking out for him, ready to receive him happily with open arms. When his father saw him from a distance, he ran and met him and welcomed him home, placed the best robe on him, put a ring on his finger, put shoes on his feet, and topped it off by having a party so the whole community could see that he had forgiven and restored his son (see Luke 15:11-32). This story denotes a re-instatement of the son's status and the father's unconditional love.

There is also a robe that symbolizes spiritual purity and righteousness where the saints who have had an encounter with God and accepted Jesus Christ as their Lord and Saviour will be wearing fine linen, clean and white, for the fine linen is the righteousness of the saints (see Revelation 19:8). When sin entered the world at the fall, sacrifices of animals and birds were offered up to God by the priest for man's sin. Sometimes, the priests themselves were found unworthy to offer the sacrifice, and some people were at a disadvantage because they couldn't afford the animals for the sacrifices. So, God, who loved us so much, sent His only begotten Son, Jesus Christ, into this sinful world to be crucified to redeem us and bring us back to Himself. Before the fall, man was perfect, living in a perfect world with no sickness, pain, or lack, and had a perfect relationship with a perfect God. Then man disobeyed, rebelled, and turned their back on God, trying to please the carnal nature.

This robe of righteousness is a divine gift from God, the Father, to humans; it is a special gift that is unmerited. It cannot be bought, worked for, earned, or deserved. This "free gift" is freely given to everyone who accepts Jesus Christ as Lord and Savior of their life. The moment you accept Jesus Christ as your personal Lord and Saviour, you become born again through faith in Jesus and are considered adopted children in the family of God. You become a joint heir with Jesus, receiving the Holy Spirit and all the benefits of sonship/daughter-ship, having an intimate relationship with God, the Father, God, the Son, and God, the Holy Spirit.

God wants you to come to Him just the way you are in whatever condition or circumstances you are; it doesn't matter your past, whether you have committed the most gruesome crime or not, or whether you are a fugitive or not. There is no sin too great, nor have you gone too far, where the hand of God cannot reach you. King David, during his time of persecution by King Saul, was constantly on the run and hiding.

Where can I go from your Spirit? Where can I flee from your presence? If I go up to the heavens, you are there; if I make my bed in the depths, you are there. If I rise on the wings of the dawn, if I settle on the far side of the sea, even there your hand will guide me, your right hand will hold me fast. If I say, "Surely the darkness will hide me and the light become night around me," even the darkness will not be dark to you; the night will shine like the day, for darkness is as light to you. (Psalm 139:7-12 - NIV).

God is omnipresent. He is present with you, and His presence is everywhere, all at once. He is omniscient, knowing all things, even the minute details of your life, and

He knows the number of hairs on your head. Remember that God saw you before creation; He is the one who formed you in your mother's womb, and He knows your needs before you even knew them (see Jeremiah 1:5).

God's efficacious blood has enough worth to ransom every man who ever lived on earth from sin. Unfortunately, not everyone will accept His gift of salvation to cleanse and make them whole.

God's provision, favour, healing, and deliverance by the death on the cross and resurrection of Jesus Christ clothed us in garments of salvation and a robe of righteousness.

To be robed in righteousness is to put on the whole armour of God. Prayer is the critical spiritual armour that keeps you alert to attacks. Prayer is talking to God and listening to Him. Prayer fosters a healthy relationship with God and man. Prayer contributes to your moral development and personal and spiritual growth. Prayer will promote a positive outlook even in challenging times, give comfort, peace of mind, and strength for the journey ahead as directed by God.

Finally, my brethren, be strong in the Lord, and in the power of his might. Put on the whole armour of God, that ye may be able to stand against the wiles of the devil. For we wrestle not against flesh and blood, but against principalities, against powers, against the rulers of the darkness of this world, against spiritual wickedness in high places. Wherefore take unto you the whole armour of God, that ye may be able to withstand in the evil day, and having done all, to stand. Stand therefore, having your loins girt about with truth, and having on the breastplate of righteousness; And your feet shod with the preparation of the gospel of peace; Above all, taking the shield of faith, wherewith ye shall be able to quench all the fiery darts of the wicked. And take the helmet of salvation, and the sword of the Spirit, which is the word of God: Praying always with all prayer and supplication in the Spirit, and watching thereunto with all perseverance and supplication for all saints (Ephesians 6:10-18 - KJV).

You are the salt of the earth. But what good is salt if it has lost its flavor? Can you make it salty again? It will be thrown out and trampled underfoot as worthless. "You are the light of the world—like a city on a hilltop that cannot be hidden. No one lights a lamp and then puts it under a basket. Instead, a lamp is placed on a stand, where it gives light to everyone in the house. In the same way, let your good deeds shine out for all to see, so that everyone will praise your heavenly Father. (Matthew 5:13-16 - NLT).

- The helmet of salvation protects the head, which is the seat of the mind, to guard your thoughts and mind.
- The sword of the Spirit is the Word of God, the Bible, which allows believers to be strong to withstand the evil one.
- The shield of faith protects believers from the fiery darts of the wicked and to trust God.

- The breastplate of righteousness protects the heart from satan's accusations and resists temptations.
- The belt of truth sets believers apart from the world with honesty and integrity.
- The shoes of the gospel of peace prepare believers to share the good news of salvation and for the challenges they may face.

QUALIFIED WITHOUT TITLE

To be qualified is to be acceptable, competent, and capable of meeting the required standard to accomplish a given task or job. To be "qualified without title" means you are considered competent for a position or role based on your skills and experience but do not officially hold the title associated with that position; essentially, you are considered competent to perform the job functions but haven't been formally designated with the title due to various reasons, for example, a temporary assignment, pending approval, or a company structure that doesn't require a specific title for that role. God will qualify the unqualified and use them for His glory. To be accepted for a task, job, or position in a group, there are specific criteria that one must meet to be deemed qualified—whether it's certifications, experience, skills, talents, or licenses that demonstrate one's ability to perform the task competently in a particular field.

When God called Gideon to save Israel from the hands of the enemy, he was a poor farmer beating out wheat in the winepress. Gideon was fearful, lacking self-confidence, and complained that he was from the weakest clan in Manasseh and the least of his family. But God chose the weak, the least of them, and a fearful man, and called him "Man of valour" (mighty warrior). Gideon was reluctant and felt he was incapable of serving, but God reassured him that his life would be spared. God equipped him for battle, and he led a troop of 300 men to victory over the Midianite army. God qualified him, and he was known as the greatest of the fifteen judges at the time in Israel (see Judges 6:1-23).

Not that we are sufficiently qualified in ourselves to claim anything as coming from us, but our sufficiency and qualifications come from God. He has qualified us [making us sufficient] as ministers of a new covenant [of salvation through Christ], not of the letter [of a written code] but of the Spirit; for the letter [of the Law] kills [by revealing sin and demanding obedience], but the Spirit gives life. (2 Corinthians 3:5-6 – AMP).

Being qualified without a title reminded me of the story of King David when he was just a little boy. After the Lord had rejected King Saul, He had chosen a new king over Israel. God told Samuel, the priest, to go to Jesse's house and anoint one of Jesse's sons. The priest poured the holy oil from the horn, but the oil would not flow; this was done to all of Jesse's seven sons. Samuel asked if these were all his sons. Jesse replied that there was a young one who had been taking care of the sheep. Samuel told them to go and get him, for the Lord had chosen him (see 1 Samuel 16:1-13). David was young and considered immature and did not have the appropriate stature for a king; however, he was the one the Lord had chosen and anointed to be king.

Little David may have been seen as insignificant and unimportant, but he was doing the best he could, tending to the sheep. While tending to the sheep, he was alone, and he had to fight bears, lions, and other ravenous animals to protect and prevent the sheep from being harmed or killed, risking his own life in the process. Little did he know, while caring for the sheep, that he was building strength, responsibility, and courage —characteristics that made him fit for a leader and a king. At the time God chose David, he was just a boy, the last of his siblings, but he was chosen for a role, not based on his current position or social status.

You may not be the most qualified, the most experienced, nor the one chosen by popular demands, but if God is for you, who can be against you (see Romans 8:31). You may have been undermined and overlooked for a long time, and maybe you are thinking if it was going to happen, it would have happened already. Perhaps it was fate because all seemed hopeless, leaving you feeling helpless, with no more strength left to fight, so whatever will be, must be. My friend, God is calling you to a life that is pleasing to Him, and He wants you just the way you are. You may not fit into the status quo with all the attributes you thought you needed to have to be accepted and appointed, but God qualifies those He calls and prepares all that will be needed for the task ahead. At the right time, God will make it happen (see Isaiah 60:22).

Paul, the Apostle, was a living example of how God qualified him without a title. Paul was known as Saul, an ardent Pharisee (a member of an ancient Jewish group distinguished by strict observance of the traditional law, self-righteous, and pretensions to superior sanctity), who studied at the feet of Gamaliel, the greatest teacher and rabbi. He persecuted the early Christians, victimized them, made evil plans against them, and even murdered them for their faith. God converted him on the road to Damascus, changing his name from Saul to Paul, and he became the apostle to the Gentiles. He became a leader in the early Christian church, writing several books of the Bible, including Romans, Ephesians, Galatians, and 1 Corinthians, to name a few, and founded many churches, spreading the gospel throughout the world. Paul testified that the gospel he preached was not devised by human wisdom but was taught directly by Jesus Christ Himself (see Galatians 1:11-2:21).

Paul said, *"Brothers and sisters, think of what you were when you were called. Not many of you were wise by human standards; not many were influential; not many were of noble birth. But God chose the foolish things of the world to shame the wise; God chose the weak things of the world to shame the strong. God chose the lowly things of this world and the despised things—and the things that are not—to nullify the things that are, so that no one may boast before him. It is because of him that you are in Christ Jesus, who has become for us wisdom from God—that is, our righteousness, holiness and redemption. Therefore, as it is*

Cavaline Colquhoun

written: *"Let the one who boasts boast in the Lord.""* *(1 Corinthians 1:26-31 - NIV).*

God sees the deep desires of your heart and the good intent you have towards God, His people, and His kingdom. You might say those were many years ago in the Bible; things and times have changed, and it does not happen anymore. You may ask, *"How does this apply to me?"*

As a registered nurse in Jamaica, I was assigned to work in a department I had never worked in before, and within six months on duty, I was selected to be the nurse in charge. I was not the most experienced nor the most qualified, but I was chosen for the role. At first, I was elated because it was a post I had always wished to hold; finally, it happened, but doubt set in. God, in His infinite wisdom, equipped me with the right skills and attitude needed for the job. He also favoured me with the best staff, supervisors, and supportive system a department needed to be effective and efficient in not only meeting the needs of patients and their families but also their spiritual needs. I was even recognized and awarded second runner-up for Nurse of the Year. Whatever your hands find to do, do it with the best of your ability as unto the Lord. Whatever you practice, you will become good at and always seek opportunities to improve.

God doesn't change, and He will never change. God is not biased, and He will do for you anything you can think of, as long as it is according to His plan and purpose for your life. You might be on the backside of the desert, where no one sees or hears you, but God sees and hears. Ask Hagar, who was pregnant for Abraham. Sarah treated her with disdain, and she ran to the wilderness alone and scared. The angel of the Lord visited her and told her to go back to her mistress and submit herself (see Genesis 16:1-9).

CHAPTER 5

How Does Your Self-Worth Influence Your Net Worth?

1. Understanding Yourself
2. What Defines Your Self-Worth
3. How Much Does Your Self-Worth Influence Your Net Worth

CHAPTER 5 SUMMARY

Your worth is not dependent on your wealth or the lack thereof.

Understanding who you are will determine how you perceive yourself, whether positively or negatively.

Your self-worth will enable you to evaluate yourself as the "good thing" you were created to be, with all the attributes of love and respect, and to receive the promises God has for you.

Your net worth is measured by your material wealth; however, you should not, at any time, feel less valuable or productive according to the status quo.

You should not value yourself by the cost/price of diamonds and pearls only, but by the many lives you have impacted in a meaningful way that will shape the lives of individuals, families, and society.

UNDERSTANDING YOURSELF

The word Greek word for "understanding" is *suniemi*, which means to put together mentally.

To understand is to achieve a grasp of nature, significance, or explanation of something (Webster's Dictionary)—to gain insight into something, interpret or view (something) in a particular way (Oxford Dictionary).

What do you value most? What is priority on your list? What is the most important and authentic first step in understanding yourself?

Refrain from comparing yourself to others and feeling inferior when you think you are not doing as well as they are or when you think you should be doing what they are doing. You may think you should look like them, but the truth is, they might be saying the same things about you. Feeling this way, though, could help you gain a clearer understanding of the fact that you are not being your true self. The moment you compare yourself with others, you automatically subject yourself to bias, distorting the way you view yourself.

This bias, whether you are aware of it or not, is a propensity to think and act in a particular way based on your limited knowledge or personal experiences. It may be triggered by your upbringing, stereotypes, and culture, which can lead to impaired judgment and negative outcomes. Bias can prevent you from learning from your mistakes and lead to self-sabotage.

If you believe you are not good enough, as we tend to avoid information we do not like and agree with—even if it is true—your brain will unconsciously filter the data, distorting your perception of truth.

Do not put anyone above or below you because the moment you do, you will distort your perceptions of yourself. You will minimize yourself if you think people are above you and exaggerate yourself if you think people are beneath you. That is why the Bible said, judge not lest ye be judged (see Matthew 7:1). You should not condemn or austerely criticize others because, by the same standard you use to judge them, you will be judged too.

When you judge others, you may see the negative of yourself, your disowned parts or, may I say, your shadow self that you suppressed for months or years like a secret or fantasy that may be in conflict with your conscious self-image. If your self-awareness is heightened excessively, it could be a sign that you are experiencing poor self-esteem and lack confidence, ability, and self-worth. Judging others may give you a false sense of comfort or superiority, but it only makes you a slave, where you would like to stop, but you are stuck in this cycle; the more you judge others, the more shameful and guilty you feel. It is like taking drugs, alcohol, gambling, lying, stealing, smoking, whatever the addiction; you need help.

When you don't fill your day with high-priority actions, then low-priority distractions, such as impulses, infatuations, and mere pleasures, will take their place. Embracing both pain and pleasure will give you a real objective in life, bringing a sense of balance. Instead of comparing yourself with others, why not compare it with the things you value the most, like your dreams and ambitions? Understanding yourself is knowing yourself and what is really important to you and your life. Whatever you focus on occupies your space, time, and mind.

Steps to understanding yourself:

1. **Identify your priorities:** Focus on the things that are most important to you (high priority).
2. **Delegate lower priorities:** things that need to be done but can be accomplished by other competent people.
3. **Have reflective awareness and own all your traits:** the ability to evaluate your thoughts, feelings, and behaviour—to examine yourself to see if what you

are harboring in your heart will hinder you or help you embrace your authentic self.
4. **Align your priorities with the Word of God:** Submit to God's will in total obedience.
5. **Pray to God:** You must be honest and have open communication with Him. Ask Him to reveal scriptures that reveal His plan and purpose for your life and to guide you in the field He wants you to venture into.
6. **Believe God:** Take Him at His Word.
7. **Repent and confess:** Be transparent. Do not withhold any secrets from God. He already knows because He is Omniscient. He just wants you to be obedient.
8. **Exercise faith in God:** Hold God accountable for His Word. Give yourself and all that you have to God, and trust Him to take care of you, provide for you, protect you, watch over you, pray for you, and fight for you.
9. **Scripture reveals:** Seek first the kingdom of God and His righteousness, and all these things will be added to you (see Matthew 6:33). The kingdom of God is where He rules and reigns in the hearts of His people. The sovereign God redeemed and delivered His people from sin and damnation. The kingdom of God is like a grain of mustard seed, seen as tiny and unimportant, yet with the potential to grow and be impactful. Similarly, a small act of faith, though insignificant, can influence and change the world (see Matthew 17:20).

Understanding is one of the seven gifts of the Holy Spirit, which helps you appreciate the mysteries of faith in God. This supernatural ability is given to believers to build up the body of Christ and advance the kingdom of God.

Psalm 57:2 says, *"I cry out to God Most High, to God who fulfills his purpose for me."* This is key to understanding God's purpose for your life. God has numbered your days and will fulfill every purpose He has for you.

To better understand yourself, you need to answer these three questions:

1. Who am I?
2. What am I doing here?
3. Where am I going?

WHO AM I?

You are created in the image and likeness of God, and God is eternal in nature with no beginning and no end. He is infinite, with no limits and boundaries of time or space. God is unchangeable. He remains the same before time, now, in all seasons and forever. Amen. You are also of an eternal nature like God.

You are a child of God (see John 1:12).

WHO AM I ACCORDING TO GOD?

- I am the righteousness of God—I have right standing with Him—in Jesus Christ (see 2 Corinthians 5:21).
- My body is a temple of the Holy Spirit; I belong to Him (see 1 Corinthians 6:19).
- I am the head and not the tail, and I only go up and not down in life as I trust and obey God (see Deuteronomy 28:13).
- I have the mind of Christ (see 1 Corinthians 2:16, Philippians 2:5).

WHAT AM I DOING HERE?

God created human beings to be a true reflection of Himself so that the world would see the character of God reflected in them. God wants us to be good stewards to take care of the environment, including the land, sea, animals, and people. We should reproduce and have godly children, obey His commandments so we can live a life of abundance, and worship Him in Spirit and in truth.

If we do not follow God's instructions and align our lives with God's precepts, we will face God's judgment and wrath. But God, in all His wisdom, love, mercy, and grace, sent His Son, Jesus Christ of Nazareth, to sacrifice His life to be crucified on Calvary's cross for all the sins of the world so that whoever believes in Him will not perish in damnation but will inherit eternal life.

WHERE AM I GOING?

There is life after we die. Those who are redeemed by the blood of the Lamb and the word of His testimony and have their sins forgiven will have a mansion in heaven that God has prepared with streets of gold.

WHAT DEFINES YOUR SELF-WORTH?

Self-worth is the core belief about your values and abilities that guides your thoughts, feelings, and actions. Self-worth is how you see yourself. It shapes your self-perception, influences your decision-making, and affects how you relate to others. Knowing you are good enough gives a sense of belonging and lets you know you are worthy of love from others. Self is individualized and personal; it's how you think, feel, and treat yourself and believe in what you know to be true about yourself, even if others do not approve.

The way you value yourself speaks volumes about who you are. Did you know people treat you according to how you treat and conduct yourself? The behaviour you accept from others will say much about your self-worth. For example, I would accept any gift that was given to me until I witnessed someone being told to select the most appropriate ones and give them to the other person, while I would receive the rest. That was an eye-opener for me because I accepted things out of humility, thinking it was the best, but I was being taken for granted. After that incident, I started to ask for specific things and became very particular about the things I accepted and the way I was being treated.

I recall that when I was growing up, I never remember getting clothes and shoes with the tags or labels still on. My mom is a seamstress, and she would make my clothes, including uniforms for school. However, when relatives gave us clothes, they were often misfitting, either too small or too big, and so Mom had to alter the clothes to fit me. When the shoes were too big, she would stuff the front and cut cardboard into the shape of the shoes, using it to line the sole so I could wear them. Children would laugh at us, saying we were wearing our bigger siblings' shoes. At times, I would wear my church shoes with heels to school, and children would stare at my shoes and say they knew it was me coming from a distance because the shoes would make a lot of noise as the tips had worn down. Many times, we would go to school barefooted. Many children in our school and community would experience the same thing. I felt so uncomfortable because other children never wanted to play with me. They only wanted to come around for me to help them with their homework.

Self-worth is often confused with self-esteem, which refers to the way one thinks and feels about oneself.

Define yourself by how you think about yourself, how you treat yourself, and how you allow others to treat you. Be kind to yourself. Take care of yourself. Don't compare yourself with others. Find inspiration in others who are similar to you, and be confident that you can handle whatever comes your way. Acknowledge your weaknesses, but don't let them define you. Learn from your errors. Accept changes as part of life; embrace them with an open mind.

Push yourself to do and be the best; don't demand perfection. Spend time with the Lord and with people who bring you happiness. Practice self-care, eat healthily, stay active, love, and do things that you enjoy, such as reading books that inspire you to take action. Enroll in courses that will help you succeed and achieve the next level. Avoid negativism that can hinder your growth and prosperity.

Self-worth is not defined by what you have accomplished, nor is it defined by what you have or what you don't have; Your self-worth is who God says you are. Seeing yourself in the eyes of the Lord will define your self-worth.

Do not compare yourself to others and feel inadequate based on perceived differences.

HOW MUCH DOES YOUR SELF-WORTH INFLUENCE YOUR NET WORTH?

Your self-worth can have a positive or negative impact on your net worth. When your self-worth is low, it can negatively impact your financial decisions. It is never good to overspend due to a feeling of inadequacy, where you feel as if you are not good enough, smart enough, or successful enough, or you lack confidence in managing your assets, including your finances. You may be fearful of taking risks and not seeking opportunities to increase wealth, which can result in stagnation or dormancy and impede growth in your net worth.

Positive self-worth is how you see yourself, that you are worthy of the best, and you desire the best and strive to be and do the best in your field. Positive self-worth will encourage you to actively seek information about financial discipline, enabling you to make informed decisions and achieve your financial goals. Some of these disciplines include creating a budget, minimizing unnecessary spending, opening a savings account, and regularly checking your debts, including your credit card balances, to ensure how much you owe and pay your balance in a timely manner to reduce added interest rates. Invest in your health and your future financial security, such as retirement plans, stocks, and bonds, to ensure financial stability and wealth accumulation.

Everything belongs to God, including you and your assets. God gave you the health, knowledge, and ability to gain wealth (see Deuteronomy 8:18), and it is your responsibility as a good steward to take care of and manage what is entrusted to your care, including your money. Wealth and money are two words that most Christian women try to sidestep, believing they must be content with what they have. Who said you should not have money? The Bible warned against the love of money, not having money or wealth. There is nowhere in the Bible where God condemns money or wealth.

For the love of money is the root of all evil: which while some coveted after, they have erred from the faith, and pierced themselves through with many sorrows. (1 Timothy 6:10 - KJV).

What is condemned is the pursuit of money and wealth, where it controls your life and becomes an idol.

Thou shalt have no other gods before me. (Exodus 20:3 - KJV).

Jesus spoke of the danger of riches in the parable to the rich man and the eye of the needle.

And again I say unto you, It is easier for a camel to go through the eye of a needle, than for a rich man to enter into the kingdom of God. (Matthew 19:24 - KJV).

Money is a universal language, and there is nothing you can accomplish without money.

The Apostle John encouraged his brethren:

Beloved, I wish above all things that thou mayest prosper and be in health, even as thy soul prospereth. (3 John 1:2 - KJV).

Wish others well in all aspects of their life, including physical, mental, emotional, and financial well-being, with an emphasis on spiritual well-being, which will determine how the other aspects of their life prosper.

The blessing of the Lord, it maketh rich, and he addeth no sorrow with it. (Proverbs 10:22 - KJV).

CHAPTER 6

Can I Really Be Whole?

1. Complete and Confident
2. Regain Your Traction (Gain and Maintain Composure)
3. How to Live a Balanced Life

CHAPTER 6 SUMMARY

In essence, wholeness matters because it promotes a life of balance, integration, and harmony.

It encourages you to see the interconnections within yourselves, among each other, and within the world around you.

By embracing wholeness, you pave the way for a more compassionate, sustainable, and enriched life.

I am redeemed by the blood of Jesus Christ from the curse of sin, sickness, and poverty (see Deuteronomy 28:15-68, Galatians 3:13).

Cavaline Colquhoun

In biblical times, women didn't have to do anything immoral or illegal or behave out of context to be marginalized. The fact that they were women meant being discriminated against. The Constitution does not guarantee equal rights and justice for women. There appears to be justice for the rich and privileged, and another for the poor and disfranchised, one for women and another for men. Some people may find justice in the clubs or on the golf course, while others cannot obtain justice within the court system. Women work twice as hard and even more to achieve and receive what is due to them as compared to men but are still not fully rewarded and compensated because they are deemed inferior and inadequate to men. Regardless of how society may have defined or redefined the role of women, you are made complete and equal in the sight of God. Hold on to this truth and know who you are and whose you are. Society may not acknowledge you, but be encouraged; they also did not accept Jesus Christ, the Saviour of the whole world. So, do not throw away your confidence; it will be richly rewarded. You need to persevere so that when you have done the will of God, you will receive what He has promised (see Hebrews 10:35-36). The Apostle Paul reminded us that in Christ, all the fullness of God dwells in a human body. So, you also are complete through your union with Christ, who is the head over every ruler and authority (see Colossians 2:9-10).

I was reminded of a story in Numbers 27:1-11, where Zelophehad, an Israelite and a member of the tribe of Manasseh, died leaving five daughters and no male heirs to claim the inheritance. The daughters were denied because they were females, and according to their custom, only sons could be successors and carry the family name. So, the daughters decided that their pursuit of receiving their father's land was so that his labor would not go in vain and his name would not be lost. The daughters went to Moses and petitioned him to give them the inheritance that was rightfully theirs. However, Moses took the case before the Lord because he had never encountered a situation like that before. He prayed, asking God to intervene, and God instructed Moses to give the inheritance to the daughters. Zelophehad's daughters then married their cousins within their father's tribe to keep the land allotment intact.

Women have been stereotyped, refused opportunities, and have been rejected certain status and credentials just because they are females. They have been treated unfairly, subservient, and underpaid, even though they are qualified and competent for the job and position. Women are not seen as equal to men; they are demarcated as a lesser gender who are not recognized, appreciated, and seen as important in certain fields. They are perceived as possessions, traded in the marketplace like goods and services, and bartered to the highest bidder for their selfish gain and desires. Significant disparities remain in how women are valued and acknowledged, depending on the cultural context and societal norms.

You may have exhausted every means you know and don't know what else to do or where else to go, but may I implore you to turn it over to Jesus. You have been fighting from a place of brokenness; now fight on your knees from a place of victory, knowing that this journey you are on is a battlefield, and the battle is not yours but the Lord's. Don't be disheartened; you may seem invisible, not being identified by your name, face, or voice, but be reminded that the God who created you sees you, knows your name and everything about you, and He loves and cares for you.

Women have a greater need to pray for their family, church, community, and government continuously (see 1 Thessalonians 5:17) and fervently to overcome the oppression that prevents them from striving and thriving through social systems implemented in society. For example, there are the caste and system of stratification, which determine social hierarchy that divides people into groups based on occupation, birth country, zip code, race, gender, and who you are related to. Many organizations put women in a secondary position and deny them prestige and honor, saying that a woman's place is in the home, even in this 21st century and beyond.

A major consensus among scholars and students of ancient studies suggests that women in ancient times were often viewed as second-class, oppressed, and subservient to men. If you have experienced abuse, rejection, lack, homelessness, helplessness, and hopelessness, and are fighting against the grade, pray through circumstances that may break you and leave you wounded. Don't give up or give in. God can turn things around in your favour. The fact that you went through so much and are still alive is enough reason to suggest that you are destined for a divine purpose. You are not alone. We are praying and interceding on your behalf. Be confident that God hears your heart and every one of your prayers, and He is bringing you out so you will be able to testify to others who need to be empowered to keep the faith. I am convinced and confident of this very thing, that God who has begun a good work in you will continue to perfect and complete it until the day of Christ (see Philippians 1:6). You may experience loss and failure—one after the other—and the doctors may not know what else to do. You may be unable to meet your basic needs, but trust the Lord, our Jehovah Jireh, to provide all your needs according to His riches in glory through Christ Jesus our Lord (see Philippians 4:19).

Don't quit. Revamp and win. You are worth it. Say it and believe it.

You may have tried everything and spent all you had, and the situation remains the same or has worsened. You might come to the conclusion that if it was meant to be, it would have been, that that is your fate, but that's a lie from the pit of hell. Let me remind you that I kept pressing. If I had given up, you wouldn't be reading this life-changing book. I was not in the best of health while penning these words for you. I was wearing a bilateral wrist brace and a back brace, doing physiotherapy, and taking dozens of medications weekly to be able to endure the pain to complete and publish this book. I had personally experienced all of the above, and it is the unmerited grace and mercy of God that has and continues to keep me. God allowed all those trials to teach and transform me into the person He ordained me to be.

Trust God with all your heart, even if there is no evidence of possible change. Trust God because of His track record. He cannot lie, and His every Word is true. Whatever He promised, He will fulfil (see 1 Corinthians 1:9).

And he believed the Lord, and he counted it to him as righteousness. (Genesis 15:6 – ESV).

For the Scriptures tell us, "Abraham believed God, and God counted him as righteous because of his faith." (Romans 4:3 - NLT).

This is my testimony: I was stripped of all I had except the clothes on my back and the pair of slippers on my feet. I didn't have an ID card to say who I was, but God. It took me many years to fight against anger, unforgiveness, and disappointment in my mind and heart, and to plead on my knees for God to intervene. I also fought the court system to be heard and to receive justice. After eleven long years, I finally received what was rightfully mine. I realized that I couldn't physically manage the warfare because it was a spiritual battle, so I had to give it all to Jesus and submit to His Lordship and authority to guide me through to the other side.

I was told many times that I should just settle for where I was and be content. After all, I was much better than a lot of people with the same health condition. I was not trying to prove a point; I refused to accept anything but the best, and I strived to live the life God intended for me. I failed one exam five times and heard the answer "No" more than I ever anticipated. I made so many mistakes with poor choices and decisions, but I've learnt my lessons well enough to teach and empower others to refrain from following the same disruptive and destructive paths.

I was called derogatory names and was told that I wasn't good enough, I wasn't going to be anything good, and I was pretending to be who I was not. Once, a very influential man came and visited me at home because I wasn't feeling well. He took out a condom, wanting to have sex with me. I refused him, only to be told I had low self-esteem and I should be flattered a man of his caliber found me attractive. I told him he should be ashamed of himself. I was ill, and before he prayed and wished me a speedy recovery, he wanted to take advantage of my vulnerability. I quickly asked him to leave and never to return. A few years later, he was charged with several counts of misconduct and was suspended from his office.

This confidence and trust in God have caused me to be resilient, persistent, and purposeful. Knowing that I am still standing gives me the determination to push past my pain, problems, and persecution to make someone else's life less agonizing and more meaningful. You too can be healed and made whole in Jesus (see Isaiah 53:5 and 1 Peter 2:24).

COMPLETE AND CONFIDENT

For in Christ lives all the fullness of God in a human body. So you also are complete through your union with Christ, who is the head over every ruler and authority. (Colossians 2:9-10 - NLT).

This means accepting Jesus as your Lord and Savior, reading His Word and following His precepts, having the desire to be like Him, living a fulfilling and successful life, sharing the good news of salvation, and reaching the lost at any cost for the glory of God.

Being whole doesn't necessarily mean you have everything and lack nothing, but to find peace in your circumstances and be content in your mind that you have free access to grace and mercy and peace in God. You are complete in your mind, body, and soul. You have free access to the grace, mercy, and peace of God the Father through the Lord Jesus Christ, and you are filled with His unfailing love. The Holy Spirit now empowers you to experience the mind and will of Christ and walk in His strength and faith.

Education, wealth, social status, and family affiliation are very important and necessary, but they are not essential for completeness. You don't need anyone to make you complete, and you don't have to be perfect to be confident.

She Fights

Believe in yourself that you are who God says you are. It doesn't mean you are self-sufficient, selfish, or conceited; on the contrary, you are totally and completely dependent on God and you are nothing without Him. Having confidence in yourself will give you the drive and the affirmation that you can accomplish whatever you were ordained to be. You are enough because God has called you and equipped you for the greater good, far beyond your wildest imagination.

As you wake up in the morning, make it a habit to read the scriptures, ask the Holy Spirit to reveal to you what you need to understand, and then pray. Listen to what the Lord has to say to you each day. The Word of God is a blueprint, a manual that will guide you through the rigors of life. You are enough because you are worthy, valuable, acceptable, and loved by God. So, when you feel that you are not enough, you may experience feelings of self-criticism and doubt. Just remind yourself of the Word of God and apply it to your life.

God wants us to stay in His presence, where He will strengthen and prepare us for whatever lies ahead, transforming our fear into confident trust.

As a woman, you have the power to choose your path—whether to remain single or to get married. The choice is yours.

If you are single, know this: you are exactly where you need to be. This is your time to love yourself, understand yourself, and embrace the truth that you are already whole. A spouse does not complete you. You are not a half waiting for another half to make you whole—you are complete because God made you.

So, while you're single, enjoy it. Use this time to get to know God deeply and to discover who you are. When you truly understand yourself, you'll be better prepared to understand and connect with a spouse—if that is what you desire. A healthy marriage is not the union of two incomplete people trying to become one but rather two whole individuals joining together to form a strong, united partnership.

Take the time to know your strengths, weaknesses, likes, and dislikes. Singlehood is not a curse—it's a gift. It's a season of independence, a time when you can live for yourself, pursue your dreams, and make decisions without needing permission or explanation. It's a time for "Me, Myself, and I," not in selfishness but in self-awareness and growth.

If you choose not to marry, embrace your single life to the fullest. Use it wisely in ministry, in business, in ways that impact others, glorify God, and fulfill your purpose.

And for those who choose marriage—enter it as a whole, confident woman—a woman who knows that she does not need anyone but God to validate her worth. Your value isn't found in a house, a ring, or a title. You are complete because you are His creation.

To be confident is to know your abilities and gifts, to understand who you are, and walk boldly in that knowledge. Confidence means trusting in God's provision—believing that He will supply your needs, guide your path, lead you to the right opportunities, and even to the right spouse if that's His will.

Confidence is knowing God is your source. He will protect you, provide for you, fight for you, and qualify you for every purpose He has called you to fulfill. He equips those He calls.

When you are confident in God, you no longer blame yourself for your circumstances. You see your value. You know you are enough—not because of what you have, but because of who you are in Christ. You can build a successful life, business, or ministry. You can rise. You can change your circumstances by changing your mindset. As your beliefs shift, your reality will also begin to shift.

To be complete and confident is to be comfortable in your own skin. It's about living realistically, being genuine, acknowledging your flaws, and still pressing forward with strength. Confidence begins in the mind. It's believing in yourself, even when resources are limited. It's being content while still striving to grow and move forward.

True confidence is using what you have, seizing opportunities—even in adversity—and walking boldly, knowing that with God, all things are possible. The possibilities are endless.

Strive. Thrive. And know this: in God, you are not perfect, but you are complete. You lack nothing. He honors His Word above His name, and with God, it's always yes and amen.

Yes—you can be complete and confident in God. You can live. You can move. You can have your being—in Him.

You will show me the path of life; In Your presence is fullness of joy; At Your right hand are pleasures forevermore. (Psalm 16:11 - NKJV).

GAIN YOUR TRACTION (GAIN AND MAINTAIN COMPOSURE)

Gaining traction is an intentional and relentless way to acquire clients. This is achieved by generating awareness of your products or services through user engagement, growing your brand, increasing market demand, and generating revenue, resulting in noticeable progress in your business, non-profit organization, or ministry.

You may have had a dream of a career path, writing books, or establishing your own business or ministry, and for whatever reason (fear or lack of resources), you have not been able to do so. Or you may have already started, but you are not having the impact you anticipated. You feel stuck and lack the energy and tenacity to move forward and grow to the next level. Gaining traction will help you align your mindset with your inspiration, gain insight, and develop and expand your ministry or business while retaining a balanced and healthy approach to your personal and spiritual life.

Here are seven steps to gain traction and be whole in your business or ministry:

1. **Have a clear vision and attainable goals:** Clearly define the purpose of your business or ministry and set achievable goals to measure your progress. For example, a part of my business is writing this book: It will instruct, empower, and motivate women to take action and achieve success.

2. **Identify Your Niche:** Clearly define your ideal clients or patients and tailor your products or services to meet their specific needs, effectively attracting and engaging them. For example, my ideal clients are women who have been denied, disappointed, and demotivated in pursuing their dreams.

3. **Develop a valuable proposal:** Communicate the benefits and advantages that are unique to your products or services and clearly differentiate them from competitors. For example, this book will teach you how to fight with God using wisdom, walk in your worth, and fight from a place of wholeness. The valuable lessons presented and packaged in this book

will save you millions of dollars, precious time, and sleepless nights in acquiring.

4. **Effective market strategies:** Build your brand awareness and generate leads by utilizing various platforms that will effectively channel your message to reach your target audience. For example, the use of Facebook, Instagram, YouTube, emails, LinkedIn, Google Ads, TikTok, face-to-face interactions, WhatsApp, and promotions (the list is not exhaustive).

5. **Build a support team:** Ensure that all team members have a clear understanding of their role and responsibilities and are held accountable. Foster a supportive environment where members can see their worth and value, and collaborate to achieve business or ministry success. For example, although this book is legally mine, it was a collaborative effort from even before the title was conceived. It involved prayers, mentoring, researching, writing, editing, receiving feedback, deciding on the cover design and content structure, publishing, and marketing so you could become aware of this book. It took fasting and prayers, sweat and tears, a feeling of quitting, but more so, you, to get this in your hands because you needed to hear this message. Communicate effectively.

6. **Authentic leadership:** Be transparent. Make decisions based on principles. Lead by example with integrity and openness, and inspire others to strive for excellence. For example, show up when you are assigned, demonstrate excellent customer service, give value for money, and hold true to your promises. Show appreciation and let your talk match your walk.

7. **Continuous improvement:** Analyze feedback and use customer data to customize products, experiences, recommendations, and promotions. For example, consider offering bundle sales by packaging several items together and selling them at a lower price than if they were sold separately.

Gaining traction is not just about toying with ideas but about putting them on paper and executing them. It's a holistic approach to business where you, as the leader, manager, or CEO, will actively manage and improve all critical aspects, including marketing, finance, customer service, team development, public relations, and overall operations, to achieve the highest profit and productivity.

HOW TO LIVE A BALANCED LIFE

Being whole doesn't mean that you are flawless, but rather accepting all aspects of yourself just the way they are. You've always heard that a balanced diet is essential for staying healthy, and living a balanced life leads to happiness and peace of mind. Living a balanced life is far easier said than done; it requires dedication of your time to include all the social, spiritual, and physical aspects of your life. Prioritizing the most important areas, such as family, health, career, worship, and self-care, helps synchronize your personal and professional responsibilities to avoid burnout, exhaustion, and hindered progress.

Aristotle was a Greek philosopher and scientist who contributed to formal logic and developed formal systems of reasoning. His idea of balance, or what was called the golden mean, was the notion that virtue, that is, behavior of high moral standards, is found in moderation between two extremes. Aristotle believed that this principle could be applied to many aspects of life, including ethics, finances, and work.

Your physical and mental health is the basic foundation on which all the other aspects of your life will be established and evolved to achieve a healthy, productive life. Humans tend to focus on the physical or material aspects of life, such as the body, career, and wealth, without paying much attention to the other parts that complete the human being.

Human beings were created in the image of God; the Godhead is tripartite, comprising God the Father, God the Son, and God the Holy Spirit. Humans are also considered "tripartite," made up of three parts: body, soul, and spirit. These three distinct parts are interdependent; when one is disturbed, the other two parts are also affected.

THE BODY

The body is the formed part of the flesh, made up of cells, the physical, functional part of a human that interrelates with the world through our five senses, as well as an inner spiritual connection (the sixth sense), spiritual insight, or awareness through faith or belief. You should take care of your body by actively nurturing and protecting it from harm because the body is the dwelling place of your soul and spirit.

Don't you realize that your body is the temple of the Holy Spirit, who lives in you and was given to you by God? You do not belong to yourself, for God bought you with a high price. So you must honor God with your body. (1 Corinthians 6:19-20 - NLT).

THE SOUL

At creation, the Lord God formed man out of the dust of the ground and breathed into his nostrils the breath of life (His Spirit), and man became a living soul (see Genesis 2:7). The Hebrew word for *breath* is *ruakh,* which also means *wind* or *spirit*. The Hebrew word *soul* is *nephesh,* which is normally used for both soul and mind. The soul refers to the whole person, encompassing both the physical being and inner life, so there isn't a distinct, separate word for the mind. The human being is the only creature created with a soul, and this makes humans eternal beings.

Cavaline Colquhoun

The Greek word for *soul* is *psyche-mind*, which has a broad application that includes the self, individual life, and life itself. The soul is considered the seat of feelings, desires, affections, and love (our heart, soul, etc). It's that immaterial part—the essence of a human—that can ascend to a higher plane of existence after physical death or be used more broadly to signify the essence of human life.

Theologians and philosophical theorists may have evidence that the souls of human beings exist; however, scientists have so far been unable to conclusively confirm this belief. To date, the soul remains a mysterious and abstract entity, which, hypothetically, involves an individual's personality and consciousness. Just like how you cannot see or touch pain, but you know it's there. Pain is subjective to the individual who is experiencing or has had the experience. It's not measurable by percentage or weight but rather by a self-reporting pain scale; a person may also express facial grimaces, body language, and guarding. The soul is real and alive, and it's the living part of our being, comprising the mind, emotions, and the will; the essence of a person's identity, allowing them to be uniquely recognized.

If "soul" is defined as a person's essence, we could safely say that God has a soul because He has a mind, will, and the ability to express emotions.

The children of Israel made an idol (a golden calf) and worshipped it when Moses went up to Mount Sinai to meet with God on the Israelites' behalf. God was very angry (see Exodus 32:1-35). God is also a jealous God.

You must not bow down to them or worship them, for I, the Lord your God, am a jealous God who will not tolerate your affection for any other gods. I lay the sins of the parents upon their children; the entire family is affected—even children in the third and fourth generations of those who reject me. (Exodus 20:5 - NLT).

God experiences sorrow:

He took Peter and Zebedee's two sons, James and John, and he became anguished and distressed. He told them, "My soul is crushed with grief to the point of death. Stay here and keep watch with me." (Matthew 26:37-38 - NLT).

God is love.

For God so loved the world, that he gave his only begotten Son, that whosoever believeth in him should not perish, but have everlasting life. (John 3:16 - KJV).

Human beings are the only created living beings that have a soul that causes us to feel guilty when we sin and which differentiates us from animals and any other creature God made. Apostle John encouraged the believers of God, *"Beloved, I wish above all things that thou mayest prosper and be in health, even as thy soul prospereth." (3 John 1:2 - KJV).*

Cavaline Colquhoun

SPIRIT

Being whole may include a sense of connection to a higher power, and this higher power is often referred to as the Holy Spirit. This Spirit is considered the breath that God breathed into humans' nostrils, and they became a living soul. The soul is the part of a person that connects with God and has an innate desire to worship God. It is your consciousness, intuitiveness, that part of us that can relate to God, wanting to know the heart and mind of God.

God is a Spirit: and they that worship him must worship him in spirit and in truth. (John 4:24 - KJV).

The spirit and the soul are like conjoined twins. Where one goes, the other automatically follows. The life a person lives, whether pleasing to God or not, will affect their soul.

So they said, "Believe on the Lord Jesus Christ, and you will be saved, you and your household." (Acts 16:31 - NKJV).

Your faith in God will determine your eternity. When you die, the breath ceases, the spirit goes back to the Creator, the body goes back to the dust in the ground, and the soul goes to be with God until the day of judgment. The soul that accepts and honour God will be spending eternity with Him, but God will reject the soul that rejects and dishonour Christ.

And the very God of peace sanctify you wholly; and I pray God your whole spirit and soul and body be preserved blameless unto the coming of our Lord Jesus Christ. (1 Thessalonians 5:23 - KJV).

To live a balanced life is to live a life centered on Jesus Christ. He will restore you to a life of holiness, healing, and wholeness, even in this sinful world.

CHAPTER 7

Discover Your Hidden Treasure

1. Unveiling the Power of Your Mind
2. What About You? Haven't You Seen Yet?
3. Dare To Be Different

CHAPTER 7 SUMMARY

Finding your true authentic self requires a mindset shift.

And be not conformed to this world: but be ye transformed by the renewing of your mind, that ye may prove what is that good, and acceptable, and perfect, will of God. (Romans 12:2 - KJV).

To discover the hidden treasure, you must ask the One who placed it there.

But we have this treasure in earthen vessels, that the excellency of the power may be of God, and not of us. (2 Corinthians 4:7 - KJV).

This treasure is your abilities, unique gifts, and talents that God has deposited in you to serve others and glorify His name.

'Call to Me and I will answer you, and tell you [and even show you] great and mighty things, [things which have been confined and hidden], which you do not know and understand and cannot distinguish.' (Jeremiah 33:3 - KJV).

UNVEILING THE POWER OF YOUR MIND

Unveiling the power of your mind is to discover the potential your mind holds; it can influence your actions and determine the trajectory of your life.

"For as he thinketh in his heart, so is he…" (Proverbs 23:7 - KJV).

A person's character and actions are directly shaped by their thoughts and beliefs.

I remember having to forgive someone who really hurt me to the core. I told myself I would never forgive this one, and God would understand why. It was one of the most difficult challenges I have ever faced. All the feelings I had were bottled up, and some were buried so deeply that I had forgotten about them until the Holy Spirit reminded me of every one of them and brought them to the surface—getting rid of lies, deceit, misconceptions, and fear. I was able to look at myself in the mirror for the first time and see that I was beautiful, and I don't mean sexy; I mean, there was this pure beauty that exuded from the inside out. The Apostle Paul reminds us in Romans 12:2, *"And do not be conformed to this world, but be transformed by the renewing of your mind, that you may prove what is that good and acceptable and perfect will of God." (NKJV).*

The word "mind" is mentioned approximately 96 times in the Bible, indicating the importance and function of one's mind. A person's mind is their intellect, which enables them to be aware of the world and their experiences, involving mental activities such as thoughts, memories, perceptions, reasoning, and emotions. The mind is interchangeably referred to as the heart or the soul.

And you shall love the Lord your God with all your heart, with all your soul, with all your mind, and with all your strength. This is the first commandment. And the second, like it, is this: 'You shall love your neighbor as yourself.' There is no other commandment greater than these. (Mark 12:30-31 - NKJV).

The Hebrew word for "mind" is *lev*, which also means *heart* (levav), and since your mind plays a critical role in your body, you should safeguard it by what it's exposed to, for it can either make you or break you.

"Whatever your mind can conceive and believe, it can achieve." —Napoleon Hill

If you can imagine and truly believe in something, you have the potential to make it happen in reality; essentially, your mindset and belief system hold the power to influence and manifest your goals and achievements in life.

The power of the mind can have positive and negative outcomes. Initiating a new journey may seem difficult at the beginning, but after the initial period, you'll realize that it wasn't as difficult as you thought. It may not be exactly as you anticipated, but you are heading in the right direction. Your mindset is one of the most influential forces that either drives you toward achieving your goals or steers you away from them. Matthew 14:28-31 shared the story of Peter, who stepped out of the boat and walked on the water towards Jesus but began to sink when he saw the boisterous wind and became afraid. That's the power of the mind.

Your mind is a hidden treasure, for out of it come the issues of life.

HOW TO UNVEIL THE HIDDEN TREASURE OF YOUR MIND

With knowledge comes choices, and with choices comes effort, which is by far the most difficult at the beginning. It's okay to ask for help. Consider getting a mentor or coach, building a support team, or finding an accountability partner who will encourage you and check in regularly to ensure you stay on track toward your goals. Create a structure that works for you, and start harnessing the power of your mind.

A shift in your mindset can have a profound impact on the outcomes you desire in both your personal and professional life. Remember, your thoughts affect every aspect of your life, whether you are aware of them or not. Every experience begins with a thought. Just one thought, when placed into action, creates a ripple effect that can become extraordinary.

Have you ever decided to purchase a course or an item online, and suddenly, ads for it appear all over your screen? Every time you log on, there it is. You hear it on television, see it on billboards, and even hear people talking about it. That's because your awareness has been opened. You start thinking and acting on what you want, and your mind automatically begins to pull you in that direction.

If your mind believes you are sick or lack the competence to complete a goal, you will likely start your day with that expectation. Whatever your dominant thought pattern may be, you will subconsciously look for reasons to affirm that belief. What happens then is a feedback loop: your thoughts direct your attention, and your attention reinforces those thoughts. This is why the practice of rewriting your thinking is essential to your success, happiness, and health.

Your mind is sometimes referred to as your brain, depending on the context. The brain develops habitual neural pathways that are associated with how we respond to situations. For example, if you have a time-sensitive task, as I did while completing this book, your immediate response might be tension or stress. That stress response becomes habitual. We train ourselves to react in the same way, even when the stress isn't warranted. It's the fight-or-flight response.

But you have the power and the choice in how you respond to any given situation (see 1 Peter 2:20). The process of choosing starts with becoming aware of how you are feeling. The next step is to examine the thought by asking: *Is this really important? What's the worst-case scenario?* If you determine the situation isn't a true threat, you can begin to redirect that feeling and create a new neural pathway.

Several years ago, after breakfast, I suddenly felt nauseous and vomited several times throughout the day. I couldn't eat or drink, and I became extremely weak and worried, especially because my period, which was due the day before, had not yet come. I was convinced I was pregnant. But when I woke up the following morning, it arrived. The mind has a way of playing tricks on you, so it's important to be mindful of where you place your thoughts.

Pray. Meditate. Read the scriptures and ask the Lord to reveal the truth to you so you can understand and interpret His Word.

Napoleon Hill's profound assertion that *"one's mind has the power to manifest belief into reality"* underpins the essence of personal success. This intertwining of deep conviction with concerted action offers a universal blueprint, suggesting that anyone can achieve greatness through dedicated application.

"Hill's philosophy bears as a testament to the profound influence of belief on achievement, assuring individuals that through the power of the mind, coupled with action, anything is conceivable and attainable."[1] [2]

"Therefore gird up the loins of your mind, be sober, and rest your hope fully upon the grace that is to be brought to you at the revelation of Jesus Christ; as obedient children, not conforming yourselves to the former lusts, as in your ignorance; but as He who called you is holy, you also be holy in all your conduct." (1 Peter 1:13-15 - NKJV).

Paul reminds us in Philippians 4:8, *"Finally, brethren, whatever things are true, whatever things are noble, whatever things are just, whatever things are pure, whatever things are lovely, whatever things are of good report, if there is any virtue and if there is anything praiseworthy—meditate on these things." (NKJV).* This instruction was based on biblical principles rather than the morals of the day because culture and society may not align with the Word of God.

The brain is the seat of the mind, where the sum of mental processes, including thoughts, feelings, and perceptions, are processed. It is a complex system that is involved in many aspects of human life, including memory, reasoning, and decision-making. The mind takes in information from the environment around us through the senses of sight, smell,

---

[1] https://www.newtonvillebooks.com/book/9781722510480
[2] https://mastermindbetter.com/tag/napoleon-hill/

hearing, taste, and touch to form ideas and solve problems. The mind is like a sponge, absorbing everything in its environment, which can affect your thought process. Factors such as diet, rest, stress, exercise, social interaction, substance use, trauma, pollution, noise, extreme temperatures, diseases, and fear can all impact your thought process. As the information and experiences are gathered, the mind evaluates them to make choices, express emotions, and store them as memories to be used at a more convenient time.

Whatever you feed your mind with, that is what it will generate. If you put garbage in, then you get garbage out. It's like a computer that analyzes and provides a result. In fact, did you know that the computer was built based on the intricacies and functions of the brain? Advances in computing raise the prospect that the mind itself is a computational system, a position known as the computational theory of mind.

WHAT ABOUT YOU THAT YOU HAVEN'T SEEN YET?

Note to self: *I knew there was much more to you than that shy girl who only spoke when spoken to—or unless you had something important to say. You were always isolated, peeking through the side of the window so as not to be seen by outsiders. You smiled even when your eyes were filled with the pain of your circumstances. You gave selflessly to those who needed or requested your care.*

If you take time to uncover your thoughts and dreams through self-reflection, exploration, and trying new things, you may discover some hidden treasures buried deep within. Listen to some of the compliments you have received over the years, as well as the criticism, and see how much of it you can transform into business and ministry—reaching and impacting millions.

What hidden treasure about yourself have you not yet discovered?

Life may have kicked you to the curb, leaving you feeling rejected and unappreciated. But may I reassure you—there is still hope, and there is a bright future. You have spent much of your life fighting from a place of despondency. Now, it's time to fight with God from a place of wisdom, worth, and wholeness. But first, you must unshackle your mind and free yourself from the prison mentality that has held you captive.

You are the manifestation of your own ideas. Until you change your thoughts, you cannot—and will not—change your life or your circumstances. As you journey through this book, I pray the Holy Spirit will ignite each word, bringing it alive in your heart, mind, and soul. May your encounter with Him spark a new mind-shift—one that leads you to discover the hidden treasure within that has long gone unrecognized.

Cavaline Colquhoun

"But seek ye first the kingdom of God, and his righteousness; and all these things shall be added unto you." (Matthew 6:33 - KJV).

This means making the things of God and His righteousness your number one priority—trusting Him completely to guide you into His divine provision for your life. This includes your career, relationships, business, ministry, and even your living arrangements and lifestyle.

God wants you to remove the barriers and limitations attached to your beliefs—beliefs that hinder you from operating at your fullest potential in life, ministry, and business. He wants you to rise to the higher calling within you—to embrace the truth that you are a leader, not a follower. The only thing you are called to follow are the unchanging principles and laws of God—His divine commands.

When God calls you and makes you His disciple, He also commissions you to make disciples—to share the gospel, the good news of salvation. He will equip you to be a leader who truly serves both God and humanity, but first, you must be a servant to submit to God's authority and those set over you by being obedient and respectful, recognizing that God is the ultimate source of power and guidance in your life. To use your gifts/talents to serve one another. To do the work the Lord has called you to with care and diligence. Being compassionate, forgiving self and one another. You will impact and empower others to grow, expand, and achieve greatness.

You will lead by example. You will lead from a place of purpose, giving people a reason to live, not from a title or position, but from the overflow of your life. Be temperate. Exercise self-control. Be respectful. Encourage others to take responsibility for their actions. Be innovative. Utilize critical thinking to conceive, develop, or invent ideas, products, or services that raise awareness, solve problems, and deliver value.

Ask yourself: How can I initiate change? How can I create a space for healing and restoration?

Do it through training, coaching, mentoring, writing, speaking, and motivating. The hidden treasure inside you is waiting to be unearthed—and the world is waiting for what only you can bring.

What you have not seen yet is something powerful, great, and life-changing; you may not even realize that you can acquire the skill or knowledge to bring it to fruition.

God is turning your pressure and pain into praise, your mud into a miracle, your mess into a message, and your fight into freedom. Your latter is going to be greater with God. Your best is yet to come. God will turn your weeping into dancing. He will raise you up so you can stand on mountains and walk on stormy seas.

Cavaline Colquhoun

*"The Lord God is my strength [my source of courage, my invincible army]; He has made my feet [steady and sure] like hinds' feet and makes me walk [forward with spiritual confidence] on my high places [of challenge and responsibility]. For the choir director, on my stringed instruments." **(Habakkuk 3:19 - AMP)**.*

Your past pain was real—no doubt about it. It may have left you paralyzed and perplexed, but what didn't kill you made you stronger. God can use those scars as a living testimony of His faithfulness throughout your journey. He can take your experience and transform it into fuel for business and ministry—to advance His kingdom.

"Thou preparest a table before me in the presence of mine enemies: thou anointest my head with oil; my cup runneth over." (Psalm 23:5 - KJV).

God will provide for you even in the midst of your difficulties—blessings overflowing—so your enemies will know that God is with you and for you.

Jesus told His disciples: *"My Father's house has many rooms; if that were not so, would I have told you that I am going there to prepare a place for you? And if I go and prepare a place for you, I will come back and take you to be with me that you also may be where I am." (John 14:2–3 - NIV).*

He promised to return for those who belong to Him. That same Jesus is preparing you now for purpose, impact, and destiny.

FIND WAYS TO BOOST HIDDEN TALENTS

It's time to explore your untapped potential. What do you naturally gravitate toward? Think of something you have excelled at in the past. Ask for feedback from those closest to you—family members, teachers, coworkers. They have observed you and may have recognized gifts you have yet to see in yourself.

Step out of your comfort zone and try something new—this could awaken hidden abilities. Engage in creative outlets, such as cooking, painting, gardening, writing, singing, and dancing—these can inspire growth in your personal life, career, and relationships.

You may have heard and believed the negative things people said about you. Maybe you have told yourself, *"If better was going to come, it would have happened already."* Perhaps the years have brought more struggle than breakthroughs. You may carry a history of lack and a list of disqualifications—just like Moses. When God called him to deliver His people from bondage in Egypt, Moses gave excuse after excuse:

- Lack of capability (see Exodus 3:11).
- Lack of message (see Exodus 3:13).

- Lack of authority (see Exodus 4:1).
- Lack of eloquence (see Exodus 4:10).
- Lack of special gifting (see Exodus 4:13).
- Lack of success (see Exodus 5:23).
- Lack of acceptance (see Exodus 6:12).

And yet, those were the very reasons God chose him—to prove that He is the One who qualifies the called.

"But God hath chosen the foolish things of the world to confound the wise; and God hath chosen the weak things of the world to confound the things which are mighty;" (1 Corinthians 1:27 - KJV).

You are special—crafted by God for a divine assignment. He equips you through His Word, your past experiences, the power of the Holy Spirit, and a supportive community.

Behind the mask I wore was a kind-hearted soul longing to be loved and appreciated. My dreams were hanging by a thread of hope. I knew I wanted more. I wanted better. I was told I loved to sit in high places where I didn't belong.

But I admired women like Harriet Tubman, Virginia Henderson, Oprah Winfrey, Maya Angelou, and Tamara Lowe—women who rose above the odds and transformed lives far beyond their time, culture, or status. A spark ignited in me. My throat dried, my tongue felt parched—I was thirsty. Thirsty for something more.

She Fights

I turned to the Lord, and the Holy Spirit led me through the pages of scripture. There, I felt the heart of God pour compassion and healing over me. I cried and cried—overwhelmed by grace. I didn't feel worthy, but He comforted me with revelation.

The more time you spend getting to know God, the more you will come to know and understand yourself. And that, my friend, is simply amazing.

You may not see the value in yourself because of past words spoken over you or the patterns you have lived through. But I charge you—dream again. And dream big.

Joseph had a God-given dream. He was ridiculed, hated, envied, and imprisoned for things he never deserved. But he carried purpose. The enemy tried to eliminate him before the dream could take root.

Search the scriptures: Moses. Job. Jacob. Esther. David. Deborah. Paul. You are no different. You carry something of great worth. The devil is afraid of what you're carrying because it's from God.

You were born to fulfill a divine plan. There will never be another Elijah, Elisha, Esther, or John the Baptist. They had their messages—and you have yours. The enemy wants to silence you so your people won't hear the message God placed in you. But now is your time.

The oil is flowing in this season—so stay alert and aligned with where God is working. Don't be distracted.

Don't be like Jonah, who wanted to withhold grace from people he believed were too wicked to be saved. But God says: *"Vengeance is mine; I will repay." (Romans 12:19 - KJV).*

You have made your own mistakes. You have fallen short too. Yet God has been merciful and gracious to you. The ground is level at the foot of the cross. So be obedient. Make yourself available. Let the Holy Spirit use you as a vessel of honor—to impact, transform, and rescue souls from hell into the righteousness of Christ.

Like Joseph, you may have gone from pit to prison to palace—not because of wrongdoing, but so that God's glory would be revealed. Yes, you may have been robbed of innocence, lied on, scarred, rejected, abandoned, abused, and mocked. But the fact that you're reading these words—and feeling them—means you're still alive.

And may I remind you: God has been protecting you all along. He allowed it all so you would see Him and Him alone. You are a miracle. You carry a message, birthed from the mud and the mess. And that message says: There is purpose in pain. Triumph in trials. Fire in fear. Freedom in failure. Love in lack.

DARE TO BE DIFFERENT

I had conducted research on the similarities and differences between humans, especially multiple pregnancies, and it was very intriguing to see that even though nonuplets share the same DNA, their fingerprints are unique to each individual, including the identical siamese twins who may share the same bloodstream and body parts. You may have the same name as someone else, share the same birth date, live in the same country, and may even resemble each other; yet, you are similar yet so different. None of your fingerprints are the same; your two thumb and eight fingers are all distinctly different. Not only are your fingerprints different from those of the 8.1 billion people in the world, but each finger and thumb also have unique permanent prints that are unchangeable. So, there is only one you with your own unique personality and individuality because God made you so.

Reminiscing about my childhood, I can remember that family members, teachers, and even people in the community would say that there was something different about me. Few would tell me, as I grew older, that I am special and that there is a call on my life for ministry and something extraordinary. I specifically remember being invited to an evangelistic crusade in a nearby community, where I was targeted and selected to contribute to that particular ministry, as I was told that the Lord had instructed me to do so. At that time, something came to mind to contribute JMD10,000. I never had that amount on my person, so I made a pledge and later honored it. The evangelist who was preaching prophesied that I was going to be rich, and the Lord was going to bless me with double for my trouble.

People would approach me, saying things like there was something about me that they couldn't put their finger on, that I was different. Others would gravitate toward me because I actively participated in festival dance, drama, speech, poems, and singing. I was very industrious and a good homemaker; others wanted me on their team not because I was brilliant but because I would not relent until the job or task was completed.

Dare to be different is a challenge to be your authentic self; do not compromise your true self to fit in with places or people with whom you do not belong. A square peg cannot fit comfortably in a round hole. Do not compare yourself with others. Follow your gut feeling—your intuition. If you are in doubt, check it out.

Remember, "no" is an answer and a complete sentence. Use it when necessary without apology. Do not feel belittled or ashamed when you stand up for your beliefs and protect yourself. Stand up for what you believe in and protect yourself and your integrity at all costs. Guard your private space and set up boundaries; it will tell you where others stop and you begin. Beware of people who may want to invade your privacy; they will take advantage of your weaknesses. You are entitled to it; you have a right to it, and you should protect your private space. You may be criticized when you are doing the right things, so be mindful of others who are insecure and selfish and who cannot enjoy leisure at your convenience.

Do not compromise your standards, nor turn a blind eye to those who binged off one's innocent sense of vulnerability and dream big. Aim for your goals; write down your vision and goals.

"And the Lord answered me, and said, Write the vision, and make it plain upon tables, that he may run that readeth it." (Habakkuk 2:2 – KJV).

When the vision is written down and then implemented, those we lead can "run" with it—and you will see it succeed.

God instructed the prophet Habakkuk to clearly record the prophetic message He gave so that others could understand it and share it as the gospel. A clear process begins to unfold when you make the vision plain.

Share it with someone you trust—someone who can help you realize your dream. Find a best friend, a confidant who has your best interests at heart. Get a mentor or coach—someone qualified to help you take the next step in business, relationships, or ministry.

Invest in yourself. Invest in what you believe in. Invest in your dream. Invest in you. Start paying attention to yourself a little more. Since everyone seems to want a piece of you, you might as well want a piece of you, too. Take time to do something that makes you happy—and do not feel guilty about it. You are worth the time, the effort, the love. Believe me—your body, mind, and soul will thank you for it.

You may have always been told to put others first, to serve others before serving yourself. But let me remind you: even Jesus took time away from the crowds to rest, to meet with His Father, and to recharge. And He was God! How much more do we, as mortal men and women, need that time?

Make the sacrifice. Plan to take time for yourself. Prepare for it. Budget for it. Add it to your schedule—and enjoy it. Taking time for yourself does not mean you are selfish, alone, or isolated. It means you are paying attention to your needs and your dreams, and syncing with your mental and emotional well-being.

Take time to laugh—and laugh loudly if necessary. Let down your hair. Smell the roses. Breathe. Slow down just a little, and you will begin to see and admire the beauty of your journey. Stay focused. Believe in your dream. Believe in yourself.

Envision the outcome—even if you aren't sure how you are going to get there. Show up. Apply yourself. Keep your eyes on the prize. Don't be distracted. Distractions aren't going anywhere—they will always be there. So be intentional.

Decide that regardless of what is happening around you, you will remain resolute.

Be consistent. Be persistent. Be determined—against all odds. You are going to accomplish. You are going to overcome. You are going to succeed.

In fact, you will impact lives, transform nations, and bring glory to God across the globe.

CHAPTER 8

Power of Resilience In The Fight

- Positively Shining Through Your Strength
- Overcoming the Fight Through Persistency (Learning From Failure)
- See Oppositions As Opportunities

CHAPTER 8 SUMMARY

In the fighting ring, your opponent's goal is to remain standing at the end—and to win. So should yours be.

No matter the distractions or the intensity of the heat, you are expected to stay the course, accomplish your goal, and refuse to throw in the towel—because winners don't quit.

The punches coming at you may feel fatal, so it's vital that you learn how to navigate your space, stay alert, and avoid unnecessary contact whenever possible.

Apply the instructions given and learn from your mistakes.

If you are knocked to the curb, pick yourself up and keep going. Your reward is worth the effort.

David encouraged himself in the Lord (see 1 Samuel 30:6).

You can do all things through Christ who strengthens you (see Philippians 4:13).

POSITIVELY SHINING THROUGH YOUR STRENGTH

The desire to see what was on the other side of pain looks like a daily motivation for me. Whatever the struggle, whatever the fight, I was still standing, so that in itself propelled me to push a little harder, especially when I didn't feel like pushing at all. There were days when I thought it wasn't worth the fight, when dark clouds enveloped the gloom of my current situation. I would constantly ask myself: *If I am struggling now, how will I go further?*

Be realistic, take care of yourself, and strive to live as healthily as possible. That sounded so soothing to the ear, but my gut reminded me that a birth needed to take place. Shining through your strength is to accept all the challenges and situations that you face as real and see how best you can adapt your mindset to remain emotionally and mentally stable. Bear in mind that you are not ignoring the weaknesses; instead, you will work to improve them to maintain balance.

Your inner strength will help you pinpoint the positives in everything that happens and allow you to learn valuable lessons from them. You can identify two or more strengths and develop them to improve and encourage yourself. Your strengths are the things that you are naturally good at, no matter how simple you think of them. Focus on what is strong, not what is wrong. You can be less stressed, more energized, and more engaging, seeking to help others with what you have and what you've acquired much more than you may give yourself credit for. Your experiences come with wisdom, knowledge, understanding, tenacity, compassion, empathy, and love for self and others.

Make notes of your daily activities, journal the blessings you receive and those you give, and see how things accumulate over time without much frustration and complaints. Embrace your unique qualities, such as being polite, patient, thoughtful, offering a compliment, sharing encouraging words, extending a hand, giving a hug, or sending a smile to make someone's day. Check up on someone you missed, visit the unwell, and be a good neighbour.

Shine the light you have inside of you and brighten someone's life and path. Be your best self and give your absolute best in whatever is required of you. Do it with excellence, as my grandmother used to tell me. She said you may never get another chance to let others see you for what you're worth. When you enter a room, your energy should attract others to you with the confidence of the Holy Spirit without needing to say a word. Shine for God. Let the beauty of Jesus be seen in you (see 1 Timothy 4:12). Be the heart and hand of God extended; be God's representative, His ambassador (see 2 Corinthians 5:20) that live love. Help others navigate the dark and dusty trail they are stuck in so they can find hope, healing, and wholeness.

One morning, on entering the churchyard, I saw a mature man looking emaciated and unkempt, but what got my attention was the pain and desperation that was all over his face. I stopped and said "Good morning," but he never responded. I was about to ask him how he was doing, but the evidence was staring me in the eyes. I told him that if he wished to speak, I would listen, and that's when he replied with a question, "Are you sure?" I certainly said I would. I quickly asked another teacher to take my class because we shared the same lesson, and she agreed. The gentleman and I spoke at length; he shared that he was overseas working and sending remittances to his girlfriend to build a house. All was well until he told her that he had been deported. He returned to Jamaica to the house they had lived in before he went overseas, but there was no sign of her, and some of his belongings were missing. He made contact with her mother and siblings several times, but they denied knowing where she was and also found it strange that she wasn't responding to their phone calls. He said that no one seemed to know where she was, so he decided that he was going back to his mother-in-law's house. If they refused to tell him her whereabouts, he was going to kill all of them and commit suicide.

I told him that I could see he was hurting, disappointed, and angry, and he had the right to feel that way. I asked when was the last time he ate and where he slept. He said he ate whatever he found and slept in a shed where some relatives lived. I asked him where he was going to sleep that night, and he said the same place; when night came, he would see. I asked him what his plan for his life was apart from wanting to kill his deceiving girlfriend, which he repeated many times. He said he wanted a job as a driver at a prominent business organization, but he needed a food handlers permit and a valid driver's license.

I took him to the nearest ATM, withdrew some cash, and gave it to him to buy food and toiletries, along with the address of the office where I worked. There, we would have more conversations on the way forward. He agreed, and I prayed for him, promising to help him as much as I could with what he needed to secure a job so he could find a place to live. He arrived at my office as planned, and I introduced him to the security personnel on duty, telling them he was my guest. However, they stood guard outside the office door as a precaution.

We discussed and checked the costs for the various items he needed. We agreed, and I gave him money to get a renewed driver's license; each time I would pray with him and pronounce a blessing over his life. A few weeks later, he returned with the driver's license, and we checked and ticked off each item on our to-do list as we accomplished it to see the progress in achieving our goals. Then, I gave him money to obtain his food handler's permit, as he had applied for the job. He returned to my office with the food handler's permit, and I could hardly recognize him. He smiled for the first time, and I couldn't hold back the tears. Comparing that moment with the first time I saw him at the church gate, it was night and day.

I told him how proud I felt, and I was happy that he decided to do the right thing, even though he was met with wrong. I told him that God had a plan for his life, and he needed to find out what that purpose was. I thanked God for what He had done for him and invited him to pray. He thanked God and me for reaching out to him, saying that no one had ever shown him such kindness before and he would never forget me. I gave him money for food and clothes because the size of the clothes he wore when he first returned to the island was now too big, as he had lost weight. He said the shoes were fine.

Before he left, we hugged, and he cried. My heart was touched in many places as I reminisced about how God provided people to believe in me enough to invest their time and resources in me when I couldn't believe in myself. It was a day I will never forget. He left to look for a job. Sad to say, I never saw him again. He did not have a telephone number for me to contact him, and I migrated to the USA. It is so satirical that I no longer remember his name; all the information I had on him was stored at the office I worked at, and I no longer have access, and most of it has been shredded. But wherever in the world he is, the blessing of the Lord is with him because I placed him in the care of the Lord and charged him to do likewise. I would really like to meet with him again to share with you all our short encounters. I wonder if he was an angel in disguise, testing me and teaching me a lesson to share in this book. I have many stories to share and many scars as evidence of my journey. I can now speak because I have walked through it; some wounds were a result of poor choices, and I used to jump to conclusions without getting all the facts. Either way, I have triumphed through the trials.

"You are capable of being strong and powerful."

OVERCOMING THE FIGHT THROUGH PERSISTENCY (LEARNING FROM FAILURE)

Many years ago, you thought your past, when it was the present, would never pass; how painful it was. You held on to the hurt for so long, trying to protect your future, which is now your present. You thought your future would be altered based on your past because you refused to leave the past behind. What you wanted to do or become may never have happened, but don't beat yourself up; if it is the will of God for your life, I guarantee it will come to pass.

May I remind you that just because you desired it does not mean it was God's will. A 24-hour day cannot accommodate both your past and your present, so take only the lessons of your past and accept that God allowed it to happen to teach you valuable lessons. The rest is not relevant to your future.

I am sure you don't even remember most of your past, so give it all to the Lord: your past, present, and potential future, knowing that God has a promise for you, and He wants to fulfil that promise with you.

Don't let your failure be the factor in formulating your future.

Blotting out the handwriting of ordinances that was against us, which was contrary to us, and took it out of the way, nailing it to his cross; (Colossians 2:14 - KJV).

The fear of failure is one of the greatest obstacles anyone has to overcome. We fear most times because of our past experiences, whether a failed plan, proposal, or promise, or a fear of the unknown. When we try to move forward, our negative mindset will want to remind us of past failures.

Many years ago, I failed an exam twice, and then I retook it and failed again. The fourth time, I thought this would be my ticket to fame, but I failed yet again. I was extremely disappointed and discouraged and grieved over my loss and failure, but as time went by, I gained composure. I realized it was not God's plan for my life, but because I spent thousands of US dollars, I kept trying. I was not fighting with God but from a place of despondency and brokenness.

My husband started a Caribbean restaurant in 2001, and after he grappled with many setbacks, including the redevelopment of the community, he struggled to survive with customers of different cultures. Inflation and construction in the vicinity of the business caused a nuisance and hindrance due to dust and noise, as well as difficulties with parking and pedestrian pathways, for a year. However, we were determined to keep the doors open. We showed up every business day, applying the principles of market research we learned from our corporate headquarters by engaging more on third-party food delivery apps, such as DoorDash and Uber Eats, which allow users to order food from our restaurants and have it delivered to their location. We would only deliver catering orders to their location and take food to the curb for customers who called in. It was our way of getting products out to customers when they were unable to come into the store. We worked long hours, from early mornings to late nights, just to prepare, cook, and package the meals in a timely manner for pickup.

Then COVID-19 came; it was an acute disease in humans caused by a coronavirus (SARS-CoV-2 virus), which was characterized mainly by fever and cough and was capable of progressing to severe symptoms and, in some cases, death. The elderly and people with underlying health conditions like immunocompromised such as HIV/AIDS, cancer, Lupus, DM, HTN, heart disease, to name a few, were more susceptible to complications. Most people infected with the virus experienced mild to moderate respiratory illness and recovered without requiring special treatment. COVID-19 was initially discovered in Wuhan, China, in 2019 and became a pandemic in 2020, which changed the way of living across the globe in every aspect, including the economy, social life, health, education, and the environment. The first case of COVID-19 was reported in March 2020, and New York City (NYC) was the first US epicenter of the pandemic. We laid off 80% of our staff, making changes according to the New York state and federal requirements. The restaurant utilized separate doors for entrance and exit, and the use of hand sanitizers, Lysol spray disinfectant, and wearing face masks was mandatory, preferably N95. There were 6-foot markers on the floor, and customers were asked to comply. Individuals seated at the same table must be members of the same party, with a maximum of ten people per table. All staff and patrons alike had to show proof of vaccination. Face-to-face interactions were discouraged to reduce the spread of the infection only in cases of emergency. There were restrictions on movement as people were asked to stay home. We were unable to assemble in large gatherings, such as schools, churches, workplaces, and at games, sports, for shopping, or visiting loved ones in hospitals, nursing homes, penal institutions, and at airports, as we had before. Technology changed the way people interact with others in their daily lives, and as a result, people adapted quickly to working remotely from home, attending Zoom classes, meetings, and church services, as well as engaging in online shopping and banking. We had to engage in internet interactions and social media, as well as gaming, to foster supportive bonds and build relationships. Regardless of what happened and could happen, we remained persistent and dedicated to keeping our restaurant's doors open for business, meeting the needs of our loyal customers and the incredible community.

Years later, I recognized what God had been showing me all along, but selfish ambitions blinded me. Being a registered nurse is one of the best career paths a person could pursue. The complexities of the nursing program make one well-rounded due to the multidisciplinary collaboration and the various fields it incorporates. Management, leadership, and training were my forte, and I was able to incorporate them successfully into my business and ministry.

SEE OPPOSITIONS AS OPPORTUNITIES

God knew that we would encounter difficulties in this imperfect world, even with our best human effort. Since the fall of man, the enemy has been trying to undermine God and is doing everything in his power to influence man to disobey God. So, God sent His only begotten Son, Jesus Christ, into this sinful world to die so that through His blood, we can be redeemed, justified, and given the gift of salvation to have eternal life. Whatever the enemy meant for evil, God turned it around for our good (see Genesis 50:20).

My first year in college was the most difficult of all three years. I worked some nights and attended classes during the day to support myself. It was a struggle to balance work, school, and church, and my GPA (grade point average) reflected just that. In my second year, I was fired from my job and decided to buy and sell the things I was giving away for free to collegemates on a daily basis. I started selling snacks, then quickly added food and other groceries as demand arose. Things went well because I had more time to study, rest, and traverse the corridors on campus, as well as sell goods to the students on the dorm. Other students approached me, asking me not to sell some items so they could start selling them too. I refused and kept expanding my merchandise.

One morning, while we congregated in the Dome (the hall where we usually gather) for devotion, we received a strange visit from our principal, who had received a letter stating that someone in our batch was selling and the guilty person should come forward. I did, and I was told to discontinue selling and concentrate on school, or I would be terminated. I hid and continued to sell most of the perishable items and gave away the rest. I was deeply disappointed; I cried, but I came to the realization that I had to comply because I did not want to be terminated from the program and forfeit the dream of becoming a registered nurse. With the money I had saved from the sales, I used it to start a partner with fellow students who lived on the dorm. I entered this partner with several hands and strategized the weekly draw, which allowed me to make my tuition payments and support myself. For added income, I made gift baskets and sold them to staff, students, former coworkers, family, and friends to help fund my education. Whatever the enemy meant for evil, God turned it around for my good, though it was challenging.

A shift in my mindset was what had propelled me to see opposition not as a setback but as a stage that was built for me to show others and myself that I can achieve. I had it in my mind, but I didn't know who to turn to for help. I had spent thousands of dollars on gurus, but they just couldn't reach me; they were too highfalutin. I thought to myself that if I did things differently, the outcome would probably be different. I tried several things in many different ways, and eventually, opportunities came, and then possibilities happened. Opposition is just a season that does not always last, though it may be tough. As Ecclesiastes 3:1 states, *"To every thing there is a season, and a time to every purpose under the heaven:" (KJV).*

Several years ago, I tried to migrate to the United Kingdom, but for some strange reason, it just never worked, as it was not the Lord's will. A few years later, I migrated to the United States of America, and I have seen how God has been integral in the process, allowing me to become a U.S. citizen at His perfect timing. It is a great country where wealth, skills, resources, technology, and people from all over the world live to advance God's kingdom here on earth.

I believe that this has been part of God's destiny and divine plan for my life, although the transition was not as smooth as I anticipated. God intentionally and strategically placed me here for His glory for such a time as this.

People have always been asking me for advice on health, relationships, career paths, and navigating life to achieve success. Therefore, I have decided to utilize the same information I currently provide for free to turn it into a business, allowing me to operate at a more professional level and achieve greater profitability for both my clients and myself. I went to the Lord in prayer, asking how to be a coach, a bestselling author, a renowned international speaker, and who my niche would be. Then, one morning, I received a vision from the Lord, saying, *"Cavaline Colquhoun, receive your people,"* but I still did not understand, as it was unclear who my people were. So, I would continue to ask the Lord about my niche. *Could it be just people? Which people?* Then I recall in Exodus 32 when God told Moses, "Your people." The children of Israel sinned against God. He was angry with them and wanted to destroy them because of their idolatry (see Exodus 32).

As time went by, I found myself gravitating to serving women like me who were denied, disappointed, and demotivated in pursuing their dreams, and thought it was too late for them to realize God's plan and purpose for their lives. I serve women who are and have been abused and are hurting silently, afraid to speak up because of who their accusers are, fearful of being stereotyped, and have tried so hard, but the obstacles are so overwhelming that they have given up on themselves and on God.

I am here to remind you that God has not forgotten or forsaken you (see Deuteronomy 31:8). He will take your mourning and give you joy, your despair, and exchange it for

His peace. He will make something beautiful out of your ashes (see Isaiah 61:3).

Let me remind you that He is the same God who called this world into being out of nothing; the same God who spoke to the barren womb of Sarah—long after menopause—and she gave birth to a son; the same God who called forth John the Baptist, the forerunner of Jesus; the same God who said, "Let there be light," and light pierced the darkness; the same God who breathed into clay and man became a living soul. He healed diseases, raised the dead, spoke peace to turbulent waves, and they became calm. Hallelujah! He has not changed.

He is the same God who allowed me to complete this book despite facing one obstacle after another. He was before the beginning and will remain through all eternity. What man sees as opposition, God uses as opportunity—to reveal Himself as the "I AM", Jehovah, the Almighty God.

Opposition, though it carries a negative connotation, may actually be a blessing in disguise. It could be a sign that God has chosen you for a divine purpose—just like Joseph. It may be evidence that you are being prepared for future opportunities, just like Ruth. Though widowed at a young age, Ruth journeyed to a foreign land where God had ordained her to meet Boaz, marry, and bear a child—becoming part of the lineage of the Redeemer of the world.

Cavaline Colquhoun

When the journey gets rough, change your shoes—but keep walking. Don't quit. Stay the course, and you will get there.

If you are open to change and willing to try new strategies, you can increase your success rate.

"I have told you these things, so that in Me you may have peace. In this world you will have trouble. But take heart! I have overcome the world." (John 16:33 - NIV).

Jesus never hid the reality of trials, persecutions, or hardships. But He gave us a reason to hope. He reassures us to take courage and have faith in Him because He has overcome the world. Through His resurrection, He remains victorious over sin, death, and every attack of the enemy.

CONCLUSION

Your Turning Point

1. Make a Conscious Decision to Take Risks
2. Step Out in Faith and Don't Be Obsessed With the Past
3. Strive for Excellence and Celebrate Each Win

A turning point is a crucial stage in one's life, where it is possible to make a conscious decision to change course, even if you are not sure how things will unfold.

Rock bottom was my place of residence for a long time and for too long. I was homeless, helpless, and hopeless, with my face fastened in the dirt. One morning, I had a vision that I was in a place I didn't recognize, but as far as my eyes could see, there were people all around. They looked sad and waved goodbye. I tried to call out to them not to leave me, but they kept going as if they couldn't hear me. I cried even more, but no one responded. Then, I asked the Lord to speak to my daughter Camille's heart and let her hear my call. I called my daughter's name again, and she quickly responded, "Daddy, did you hear Mommy calling?" and he said, "No." He held her hand and pulled her in the direction they were going away from me. I kept calling her, and she said, "Daddy, can't you hear Mommy calling?" But he replied, "No," and took her hand with force. Still, she was persistent. She said, "Dad, did you hear? Mommy needs me." Immediately, she pulled her hand away from his and ran back to where I was. He followed her. But when he reached me, he called out my name so loudly. Before I could respond, he placed his hand over my mouth and nostrils. I couldn't speak—I couldn't breathe. Then my daughter cried out, "Leave Mommy alone!" She said, "Come, Mommy." And at that moment—I woke up from my sleep.

I blamed myself for allowing all the trauma and misdeeds I had gone through. I was furious with God for allowing it to happen. I was so angry; I remember thinking that if I could catch Him, I would squeeze and break His neck. *Forgive me, Lord—for I knew not what I was saying.*

I was angry. Bitter. Sad. Empty. Lonely. Frustrated. Afraid. Disappointed. Everyone I asked for help turned me away. I trusted no one—nothing—not even the shadow after dark. I guess I didn't know how to relate to people anymore. Others thought I was paranoid or hallucinating. They couldn't understand that I feared my ex wanted to harm me.

I would hide in my room, lock all the doors and windows, and draw the curtains so no one could see inside. I stayed in the dark, afraid to turn on the light—lest someone saw it and knew I was there. I wouldn't answer the phone if I didn't recognize the number. I would throw out food that looked suspicious or had my name on it. I kept remembering when someone had once tried to poison me.

Every time I got close to people, I ended up hurt. So the safest thing seemed to be staying away from people altogether. The ones I trusted most were the ones who took advantage of my weakness and vulnerability. I was naïve— I believed that adults were trustworthy. I took their words as gospel without a second thought, until reality hit.

I became rebellious. I sought self-gratification—doing whatever made me feel happy in the moment. But I didn't realize I was walking a road of self-destruction. I got into relationships I had no business being in. I hurt people who didn't deserve the pain I caused.

I bargained with God. I'd say, *"If You do this for me, I'll serve You for the rest of my life."* I made that promise so many times, only to repeat the same mistakes again.

"To every thing there is a season, and a time to every purpose under the heaven: a time to be born, and a time to die; a time to plant, and a time to pluck up that which is planted; a time to kill, and a time to heal; a time to break down, and a time to build up; a time to weep, and a time to laugh; a time to mourn, and a time to dance." (Ecclesiastes 3:1-4 - KJV).

Cavaline Colquhoun

The time has come to do something different—anything, as long as it's not what you've been doing. Because what you've been doing isn't working.

You're tired. Sick and tired of being sick and tired. You've been doing all the wrong things, looking in all the wrong places. Settling for people and things that claim to mean you well, who say they have your best interest at heart—but nothing seems to work in your favor.

PAUL THE APOSTLE, CALLED BY GOD

But I certify you, brethren, that the gospel which was preached of me is not after man. For I neither received it of man, neither was I taught it, but by the revelation of Jesus Christ. For ye have heard of my conversation in time past in the Jews' religion, how that beyond measure I persecuted the church of God, and wasted it: And profited in the Jews' religion above many my equals in mine own nation, being more exceedingly zealous of the traditions of my fathers. But when it pleased God, who separated me from my mother's womb, and called me by his grace, to reveal his Son in me, that I might preach him among the heathen; immediately I conferred not with flesh and blood: Neither went I up to Jerusalem to them which were apostles before me; but I went into Arabia, and returned again unto Damascus. Then after three years I went up to Jerusalem to see Peter, and abode with him fifteen days. But other of the apostles saw I none, save James the Lord's brother. Now the things which I write unto you, behold, before God, I lie not. (Galatians 1:11-20 - KJV).

Pursue with God, follow your dreams without apology. Conquer by force, defeating and mastering your craft. So, you can be victorious and gain control over the affairs of your life. Step out of the boat in faith and trust God to take you to new heights and unknown territory. Strive for excellence, learn from every struggle, and celebrate every win, because you are a woman of wisdom, worth, and wholeness.

About the Author

Cavaline Colquhoun is a registered nurse by profession, a philanthropist, entrepreneur, coach, speaker, author, mentor, mother, and grandmother, who hails from the beautiful parish of St. Mary, Jamaica, W.I.

She has been a dedicated servant of God for the past thirty years, serving on the children's ministry board, praise and worship team, choir, and medical team.

She has a special love working with women, especially those who have been struggling to survive and strive to empower themselves and to achieve success.

Coach Cav is a humble and caring individual who is highly respected and admired by her peers and those whom she serves.

She is a giver and embraces anyone regardless of how they look or where they are from.

She believes that every woman who is given an opportunity and chooses to succeed will excel above expectations and become a woman of wisdom, worth, and wholeness, advancing the kingdom of God.

References

1. Forensic Science Simplified. Fingerprint Analysis: Introduction. https://www.forensicsciencesimplified.org/prints/Fingerprints.pdf (2023).

2. National Institute of Neurological Disorders and Stroke. https://www.ninds.nih.gov/health-information/public-education/brain-basics/brain-basics-know-yourbrain#:~:text=The%20brain%20is%20the%20most,qualities%20that%20define%20our%20humanity. Last reviewed on July 17, 2024

3. Canada Newswire Xerox Marks Human Rights and Environmental Progress in Annual Citizenship Report Press release (accessed on December 24, 2024); Available online: https://en-news.xerox.ca/news/CAN_News_11_12_2007

4. World War II Army New Testament signed by Babe Ruth (2023). https://www.museumofthebible.org/newsroom/museum-of-the-bible-to-honor-veterans-and-miltary-2023

5. Ryan McGrady is a senior researcher with the Initiative for Digital Public Infrastructure at the University of Massachusetts at Amherst and a researcher with Media Cloud and the Media Ecosystems Analysis Group. https://www.theatlantic.com/technology/archive/2024/01/how-many-videos-youtube-research/677250/

6. Cleveland Clinic (2025). Conception: Fertilization, Process and When it Happened. https://my.clevelandclinic.org/health/articles/11585-conception

7. The Computational Theory of Mind - Stanford Encyclopedia of Philosophy, (Oct 16, 2015). Stanford Encyclopedia of Philosophy - Stanford University. https://plato.stanford.edu › entries › computational-mind

8. Oxford Language Dictionary (2025). Battle definition. https://languages.oup.com/google-dictionary-en/

9. Wimer, R. (2024). Heart, mind, and soul…what's the difference? by Robert Wimer |Published March 9, 2024. heart-mind-and-soul-whats-the-difference. https://robertwimer.com/heart-mind-and-soul-whats-the-difference/#:~:text=The%20distinction%20between

%20these%20terms,worship%20and%20love%20of%20God.

10. Merriam-Webster Dictionary (2025). Battle definition & meaning. https://www.merriam-webster.com/dictionary/battle

11. When New York City was the COVID-19 pandemic epicenter: The impact on trauma care. Reviewed by: Anna Liveris 1, Melvin E Stone Jr 1, Harley Markel 1, George Agriantonis 1, Marko Bukur 1, Sherry Melton 1, Valery Roudnitsky 1, Edward Chao 1, Srinivas H Reddy 1, Sheldon H Teperman 1, James A Meltzer 1. Bronx, New York. PMCID: PMC9322893 PMID: 35881035. https://pmc.ncbi.nlm.nih.gov/articles/PMC9322893/

12. Understanding the mind | Department of Psychology (mar 8, 2016). Cornell Psychology Department. https://psychology.cornell.edu › news › understanding-m...

13. Clark, A. 1998. Being There: Putting Brain, Body and the World Together Again. MIT Press. https://mitpress.mit.edu/books/being-there

14. Dix, A. (1992). Human issues in the use of pattern recognition techniques. In Neural Networks and Pattern Recognition in Human Computer Interaction

Eds. R. Beale and J. Finlay. Ellis Horwood. 429-451. http://www.hcibook.com/alan/papers/neuro92/

15. Health and Science, (2020). New York to impose curfew on restaurants, bars and gyms as Covid worsens across the U.S. Published Wed, Nov 11 20202:01 PM ESTUpdated Wed, Nov 11 20205:07 PM EST. thumbnail. Noah Higgins-Dunn @higginsdunn. https://www.cnbc.com/2020/11/11/coronavirus-new-york-to-impose-curfew-on-restaurants-bars-and-gyms.html

16. Int J Environ Res Public Health. 2021 May 25;18(11):5645. doi: 10.3390/ijerph18115645. Beyond the Pandemic: COVID-19 Pandemic Changed the Face of Life. Shaden A M Khalifa 1,*, Mahmoud M Swilam 2, Aida A Abd El-Wahed 3, Ming Du 4, Haged H R El-Seedi 5, Guoyin Kai 6, Saad H D Masry 7,8, Mohamed M Abdel-Daim 9, Xiaobo Zou 10, Mohammed F Halabi 11, Sultan M Alsharif 12, Hesham R El-Seedi 2,13,14,* Editor: Robin Haring. ttps://pmc.ncbi.nlm.nih.gov/articles/PMC8197506/

17. Beware the dangers if cognitive bias (2023). National Commission on Correctional Health Care. https://www.ncchc.org/beware-the-dangers-of-cognitive-

bias/#:~:text=Cognitive%20bias%20in%20all%20it s,distorting%20our%20perception%20of%20reality.

18. The Computational Theory of Mind - Stanford Encyclopedia of Philosophy

19. Stanford Encyclopedia of Philosophy - Stanford University https://plato.stanford.edu › entries › computational-mind

www.ingramcontent.com/pod-product-compliance
Lightning Source LLC
Chambersburg PA
CBHW060523090426
42735CB00011B/2339